WORKING WITH

YOUR SOUL

WORKING WITH
YOUR SOUL

Ruth White

PIATKUS

Copyright © 2007 by Ruth White

First published in Great Britain in 2007 by
Piatkus Books Ltd
5 Windmill Street, London W1T 2JA
email: info@piatkus.co.uk

The moral right of the author has been asserted

A catalogue record for this book is available
from the British Library

ISBN 9 780749 92745 5

Text design by Briony Chappell
Edited by Jan Cutler

This book has been printed on paper manufactured
with respect for the environment using wood from
managed sustainable resources

Typeset by Action Publishing Technology Limited, Gloucester
Printed and bound in Great Britain by
MPG Books Ltd, Bodmin, Cornwall

In memory of my brother, Philip, with love and thanks
for all you gave and all you taught.

CONTENTS

ACKNOWLEDGEMENTS

I should like to thank my publishers and editors for all their help and support.

The groups I teach contribute immeasurable help and enthusiasm for my work, as well as inspiration by asking the right questions at the right time.

Although names and details have been changed, the personal stories told in this book are included only because of the generous permission of clients and friends.

My Jack Russell, Jackson, who has been acknowledged in other books for being beside me as I write, sadly died two years ago. I now have a Jack Russell cross bitch, called Bracken. She is still young, but also likes to sit beside me as I work.

Most of all, of course, I thank my well-known and well-loved discarnate guide, Gildas, without whose teaching, wisdom and patience none of my books could have been written.

INTRODUCTION

Over the years, I have written a number of books about spiritual and soul matters (see Bibliography) and in each one I have included details of my personal life story because it essentially informs the work that I do and the belief systems I hold. For each book, I have tried to give this personal story a slightly different emphasis or perspective, not only because I want to avoid repetition but also because different parts of my own story may have a specific resonance to the subject I am exploring. For this introduction I would like to explain what I believe 'working with your soul' means, using my personal experiences to put the material in the book into context.

My life has had a particular momentum and direction that I could not ignore. This has led me to complain from time to time that I felt I had little choice or freedom in designing its course. From the age of at least 19 years old, I felt that I had a clearly defined soul service or purpose, which has determined and shaped the way I journey. Signposts that I could not ignore already seemed to have been set in place along my path.

In many ways, my life has been extraordinary. For as long as I can remember, I have been aware that there is another presence or being with me who is not incarnate but from some subtle world that interpenetrates with the known physical world. From as young as three years old, I sensed a tall, white, shining being that for many years I felt must be an angel.

When I was 18 years old, I came to realise that this presence was a discarnate guide, with whom I could communicate. He asked me to call him 'Gildas' and to learn to become a channel for teachings and perspectives that he wanted to communicate from his discarnate, or spiritual, dimension. At the time, I was training to become a teacher of young children and I had little idea as to how I might combine teaching with being able to be of service to Gildas or the subtle worlds (those dimensions beyond our visible world where guides, angels and the after-life exist). However, it seemed that I had little choice but to try, and it was quite amazing how I found the right contacts or how openings appeared as a result of my willingness to work with this other dimension to life. After a series of challenges and synchronicities I started training as a teacher at The City of Leicester Teacher Training College, but I was a student who was desperately in need of help at a psychological level. Although today we are used to the idea of counsellors being available for students, in 1956 there were only two pioneering student counselling services: one was based at the London school of Economics and the other, Dr Mary Swainson, just happened to be at the University of Leicester. Dr Swainson was a Jungian psychotherapist but also, as she only later revealed, an inner brother of an esoteric group known as The White Eagle Lodge. She was therefore well experienced in spiritual and soul matters, as well as in the phenomenon of channelling – a very new territory for me. She long continued to be my mentor and confidant and eventually we wrote books together and have kept in touch ever since.

Mary helped me to understand more of myself and about my relationship to Gildas and the work we could do together. As the phase of much-needed therapy ended and my work with Gildas grew and expanded, Mary and I frequently worked together. The teachings of Gildas became widely circulated and a publisher invited us to write about how they had developed; eventually we co-authored three books for that publisher (see Bibliography: *Gildas Communicates*, *Seven Inner Journeys* and *The Healing Spectrum*). I went on to write several books in my name alone and was invited to conduct workshops and run groups in the UK and abroad.

Teaching infants was not my primary love in life and I later retrained as a transpersonal psychotherapist. I continue to channel

Gildas, and still maintain a practice for individuals who come for healing, channelling or psychotherapy. With the generous permissions that people are almost always ready to give, I have drawn on my experience with groups and individuals to provide the case histories in this book, although names and some details have, of course, been changed to preserve anonymity.

Although from time to time I complain of constantly meeting signposts that are too clear for my liking or temperament, I have found in the course of my work many others whose main dilemma is just the opposite. They feel that there is too much choice and no clear signposts. A common phrase I hear from those who come for therapy or consultation is, 'If only someone would tell me what I should be doing with my life, then I could get on and do it.' I have been lucky enough to find and follow my soul service, and, through this book, I hope to help anyone who has asked that question and not yet found an answer. *Working with Your Soul* will help you define your soul's purpose and enable you to follow the path you were meant to take in this life.

The search for greater meaning in life is often about wanting to serve a clear purpose or find distinct work to do. Within this desire, whether it has been expressed in such terms or not, is the longing to know what you are here for, and what purpose your soul has for you in bringing you into being on earth. Your soul is part of the search for integrity and meaning but there are times when you need help so that you can read the clues in life that will help you to work more consciously with it, and this is where this book and my work come in.

Obviously, in writing a book called *Working with Your Soul* I am coming from a perception or belief that something called 'soul' has both plan and oversight for each person's life, which is why I want to help you identify yours. This 'something' is beyond the personality that lives out its life on earth. In using the phrase 'the soul's code' James Hillman (see Bibliography) suggests that in order to know more about working with your soul you need to be able to decode its messages. The search for meaning and purpose will surely touch you at some time in your life and may lead you to religious, spiritual or psychological exploration – or maybe a combination of these. When exploring you might describe yourself as being in a phase of 'soul searching'.

My soul service has been clearly defined by having the opportunity to work with Gildas. I have worked with him as his channel or amanuensis for 50 years and will continue to do so for as long as I am able. Soul work, however, or working with your soul, is far more than any specific task or calling. While soul *service* may be defined clearly as something such as the call or will to teach, nurse, or practise law, for example, soul *work* encompasses the whole of life and the way you live it. It is the collection of tasks, challenges and experiences that life brings you in order to shape and develop you. When working with your soul becomes an acknowledged or discerned factor, life takes on a greater meaning and weaves itself together more congruently and cohesively. Thus soul service and more generalised soul work are linked, but not one and the same thing. Soul service is a direction in life, whereas soul work brings change to the way you live and make choices and decisions, and relates to the way you *grow.*

My soul service, with Gildas, has not needed much decoding. Rather, it has been dependent on a willingness to cooperate, and to a certain extent to 'go out on a limb'. I describe this part of my life as 'extraordinary'. In one sense it is a vocation or calling. In your own life you may, or may not, recognise a call to a specific defined or designated service on behalf of your soul.

Many of my clients are searching for that call, as I am sure are many of you. But vocation and definition of a certain career or direction in life is not the answer to understanding your true soul work. This comes from a deeper understanding and decoding of the soul meaning that is held within the everyday, ordinary or mundane areas of life. When this decoding is happening you can benefit more fully from the dimension and perspective of your soul and learn to acknowledge its support in every area. The ordinary and the extraordinary parts of anyone's life show the soul's intentions as if they are bright reflections from a faceted jewel. In many lives, or in certain of life's passages, the extraordinary is so intricately woven with the ordinary that it is necessary to learn how to let the light find the facets of your jewel so that you, as well as others, can see and let shine the brilliance that is surely there.

I presently call myself a 'spiritual consultant', and continue with my work as a transpersonal psychological counsellor and psychotherapist. Transpersonal psychology aims to add the dimensions of soul and spirit to psychological work so that life can be experienced as a journey that is under the care of your soul. In the first chapter I shall attempt to define the soul more clearly – it is certainly an overseeing and eternal aspect of your being. When you are more aware of and in touch with your soul, your present life purpose and the nature and meaning of the lessons you are learning become more accessible.

I believe that your present life is whole in itself, as well as being a chapter in a wider continuum of evolution. You are, therefore, an ambassador for the continuing evolution of your soul. I also believe in reincarnation and a particular organisation of the soul, which I explore further in Chapter 2. Briefly, Gildas teaches that reincarnation is more complex than one personality living over and over again; the wider picture consists of *different* personalities incarnating in order to bring balance, consistency and continuity to the soul's experience. Therefore each incarnate personality is an ambassador for the soul or a link in the chain of a continuing story. Learning to decode more about what has preceded your particular link in the chain is a major aspect of soul work (see Chapter 3).

In my experience, setting your life in context with this wider picture can be meaningful and exciting. These are the qualities that I hope I can help you bring to the journey you will take as you read the theory and wealth of personal stories contained in this book. There is a linked series of exercises in each chapter that can help you to attain a more vibrant connection with your soul, and I hope you will work through these to help you on your journey.

While working with your soul in this way you will enjoy the

experience of being accompanied at every moment by the beautiful essence that *is* soul. *Before* this happens you may often have felt like an unaccompanied traveller in an alien land, not knowing yourself and not known, seen or heard by others. It is my hope that this book may help to lead you from any sense of meaningless or puzzling *disconnection* as to where you stand in the scheme of things to an ever-present sense of meaningful *connection* and soulful living.

1

Soul and Spirit

We can use images to describe the relationship between the soul and the spirit to help us understand their differences and how they work together in a perfect partnership.

What is soul and what is spirit?

An image of a golden flame burning brightly in a silver chalice is often used when speaking of the soul and spirit and the relationship between them: soul is the chalice and spirit the flame that burns within it. This is an appropriate image to use to differentiate between the soul and the spirit as well as illustrating their relationship.

Chinese philosophy refers to the complementary principles of yin and yang (see Glossary, page 176). Using this terminology, the soul is generally assumed to be yin, or feminine principle, whereas the spirit is yang, or masculine principle. Symbols related to the feminine or yin principle are often cup-like, or hollow and containing, and silver is considered to be a feminine-principle metal. Symbols related to the masculine or yang principle are straight, phallic and penetrating, with gold as the metal of the masculine principle.

The silver moon and the golden sun – the luminaries that rule our day and our night – are considered to be feminine and masculine principles respectively and are also symbolic of the relationship between the soul and spirit: the moon is soul and the sun is spirit.

By being born, you become incarnate – a being clothed in flesh. The subtle essence that is your spirit, and which gives you much of your individuality and fire or passion in life, is very present in the incarnate 'you'. Your spirit is the active, animating principle of your higher being, incarnate within you. It is what makes you spiritually alive. You also have a soul, which exists on the higher planes and watches over and plans incarnation, rather than being animatedly present in the same way as your spirit. Soul is the receptive aspect of your higher being, but it is also an astute planner. Its purpose is to evolve, or to reach a state where depth and breadth of incarnate experience makes it wise. In this way, your soul has a purpose – or perhaps a series, or programme, of purposes – for you as you live your life. As explained in the Introduction, your soul may have a specific service for you to do, but it also plans your life in intricate ways, so that you can learn from every eventuality that life brings to you. The spectrum of opportunity and potential experience in life can seem very wide or dependent on chance, but as we shall see in subsequent chapters, the overall life plan of your soul, for you in your present incarnation, ensures that you carry on with, or balance, things that have happened in previous incarnations. Because the system of the soul is complex, the purposes of our souls need decoding so that we can do our soul work with greater success and awareness. Your soul watches over your incarnate experience but stays on another subtle plane in order to be able to do this (as explained in Chapter 2).

A perfect relationship

Your soul becomes heavy with the burden of experience, but it gradually processes all that you learn in incarnation into wisdom and wholeness. When this process is complete, it is as though your soul and spirit have attained a marriage. This is the state sometimes referred to as 'the mystical marriage'. The image of the golden flame of your spirit, burning within the silver chalice of your soul is one of soul and spirit in perfect relationship. The flame of your spirit burns away all heaviness from the silver chalice of your soul, which then contains and reflects your spiritual flame as they enter an everlasting harmony.

Carrying the image of the golden flame of your spirit burning steadily in the silver chalice of your soul can be helpful to hold in your mind as you embark on the tricky task of defining and knowing these numinous aspects of your being and consider the goal of learning to work in greater consciousness with your soul in your everyday, here-and-now life. At the end of this chapter there is an exercise using this symbol to help you to reflect more deeply on what the quality of your soul might be.

In summary then, the golden flame and the silver chalice represent your soul and spirit in perfect relationship. Your soul's vessel is clear and beautiful, your spiritual flame is non-consuming but bright, moving and unquenchable. The vessel is yin, or the feminine principle, and the flame is yang, or masculine principle. When you are in harmony with yourself and with life, your soul and spirit are also in harmonious balance.

Where does the higher self fit in?

If you are familiar with some spiritual and esoteric terminology, you might already be asking such questions as, 'What about my higher self?' 'Is it another name for soul or spirit, or is it something separate?' In the theoretical framework used here, your higher self is part and parcel of your soul and is considered to be the voice of the consciousness that oversees, processes and makes choices for the many facets of your incarnate life and existence. Your soul, your spirit and your higher self are interactive subtle aspects of your greater or wider being.

The paths of wholeness and perfection

Your soul/higher self arranges your pattern of incarnation and evolution, and decides, at the time you are born into each given lifetime, what kind of incarnation is needed or necessary to continue your eternal learning process. When you die, your spirit, or essence, returns to your soul so that the most recent learning can be integrated. Your higher self organises this integration. When your soul's need for learning through incarnation is over, your soul and spirit are totally reunited, as in the image of the flame of your spirit burning brightly within the clear chalice of your soul. Your soul does not seek perfection but the wide experience that leads to wholeness and wisdom.

Many of you will have experienced religious, ethical or moral codes based on a hierarchical model of standards and these codes imply that as you endeavour to reach those standards you are being judged and graded. Somewhere within the imagination of most people brought up in a Christian tradition there is a picture of a judgemental God sitting on a throne, holding a large record book of sins. You may have been told that if there are too many of these listed under your name you will be sent to hell.

Against this threat your hope can only be that you might manage to get a compassionate evaluation and gain entry into heaven. If you are very conscious of this idea you may spend your life doing the things and making the sacrifices that hopefully will lead you surely and certainly on the path to heaven. With such a belief you would be endeavouring to follow a path of perfection and conceiving the meaning of evolution as being about passing tests and getting better and better.

In contrast, a belief where you have a more conscious way of working with your soul sees things as spiral or circular rather than linear and hierarchical. In this way, learning from experience results in honouring ethical and moral standards of being and humanity because they come naturally from your heart and not from some outer imposition by a higher authority. Living your life to the full and embracing a wide experience with consciousness helps you to give birth to wisdom and the ability to make clear choices. Belief in karma and reincarnation sees working with your soul as being about balancing polarities and gaining wide experience of all that incarnation has to offer, so that you learn to live with compassion, insight and an ability to think symbolically about the nature and purpose of being. It is these themes that this book aims to explore and explain in greater depth and to practical purpose.

The exercise below will help you to explore working with your soul. It is based on the image of the flame of the spirit burning brightly in the chalice of the soul. Before you start, however, and before working on each exercise through the book, read the following guidelines.

Preparing for the exercises

1. Before you begin any inner-journey, or meditative or mentally reflective exercise, try to set aside the time needed for the exercise when you will be undisturbed.

2. Prepare the room in which you will be doing the exercise, so that you feel comfortable. You may need extra cushions or blankets for comfort or warmth. At the beginning of each exercise you will be told which materials, such as notebooks, crayons or sheets of paper, to have available, so put these conveniently to hand before you begin.

3. If you are intending to work through the sequence of exercises given in this book, it is a good idea to have a special notebook in which to record your experiences and reflections. Good-quality paper that is either blank or alternately blank and lined pages is best so that you can record your drawings as well. Try to have a book of a good size, giving you space to record freely and imaginatively.

4. If you can, switch off the phone. For some exercises, such as the first one, you might find it helpful to play some quiet or meditative music in the background.

5. You might also find it useful to record the instructions for an exercise onto a tape recorder so that you can listen to them rather than trying to remember each stage or needing to look constantly at this book.

6. When everything is ready, sit or lie in a comfortable posi-

tion on the floor or on a chair, bed or sofa.

7. It's best not to lie down if you associate lying down too strongly with going to sleep, but otherwise it is a perfectly acceptable position from which to work.

8. You need to be relaxed for these exercises, but not sleepy. There is a difference between the relaxation that comes before sleep and the relaxation that enables the creative part of your mind and being to come forward so that you become alert and uncluttered by outer concerns.

9. The position in which you sit or lie needs to be one where you feel comfortable and have the support your body needs. Also, your body needs to be symmetrically arranged.

10. You can cross your legs if you are sitting in a cross-legged, upright position, or in a lotus or semi-lotus position, but otherwise do not cross your legs at the knees or ankles and do not fold your arms or link your hands. A symmetrical position balances you energetically as well as physically and helps you to let go of any bodily tensions.

11. At the end of a meditative or reflective time, including intuitive drawing exercises, try not to rush into whatever daily practical tasks may be awaiting you. Instead, spend a little time allowing yourself to stretch, drink some water or tea and to re-focus to your everyday life. Especially if you have to go out into a very different environment, imagine that you have a cloak of light with a hood right around you. When you meditate or do exercises to get in touch with yourself, you can become too open or sensitive for the normal levels of everyday living and interaction. Visualising a cloak of light with a hood of light around you helps to keep all your sensitivities protected and also makes sure that you take your own light with you, wherever you go.

Exercise 1: *meditative exercise on the communion between soul and spirit*

1. Find your comfortable position (see above).

2. Focus on the rhythm of your breathing. Be aware of each in-breath and out-breath, not trying to alter its tempo in any specific way, but allowing it to find its natural flow.

3. Sense your breath as coming in and out at the 'petals' of your heart centre or chakra (life energy centre, see Glossary). This lies in the centre of your body and aura on the same level as your physical heart. (For more information on auras and chakras see Bibliography).

4. As your regular breathing helps your heart chakra to open, get a sense of entering your own inner space or dimension.

5. Visualise the symbol of a flame burning in a clear chalice.

6. Note how your flame burns and what colours it may reflect or have within it.

7. Note the shape, colour and clarity of your chalice.

8. Contemplate your chalice as the quality of your natural soul.

9. Contemplate your flame as the quality of your indwelling spirit.

10. Remain centred in this contemplation for not more than ten minutes.

11. Gradually return to your awareness of your breath in your heart centre or chakra.

12. From this awareness return to a full awareness of your whole physical body and particularly to your connection with the ground.

13. Visualise yourself as wearing a cloak of light with a hood.

14. Become aware of your surroundings and slowly come back to normal everyday consciousness.

15. Before you resume your normal tasks, take some time to draw and/or to write about your own personal image of the flame of your spirit that burns within the chalice of your soul.

2

Your Soul's Journey

By the very act of being born, you are working with, and for, your soul. The crux of the matter is whether you go on working 'blind' or whether you decide that you want to acquire more awareness of your soul's plan in order to become a co-creator in your joint evolutionary journey. If you decide on the latter, you also gain the tools to take your present lifetime more in control so that you live with a more vital sense of meaning and higher purpose. Before moving on to examples, illustrations and the personal stories of individuals, I would like to help you, through a series of analogies, towards an understanding of your place in the world and the shape of your life journey.

Understanding your place in the world

Your soul/higher self is active in making choices for your life. It observes and correlates what you are learning throughout your present incarnation and sets it in context with what has been learned in previous lives. Gradually, as the soul's evolution progresses, each incarnation begins to carry with it a 'soul contract' or an agreed programme of things that still need to be learned, experienced or balanced out with what has gone before. This programme will include the opportunity to have completely new experiences, but also to redress imbalances that may have been created in previous lifetimes.

Previous lifetimes

The concept of a soul contract assumes a belief in many lifetimes that are part and parcel of the process of achieving evolution. The choices for any given lifetime are not random but are the result of careful planning on the part of your soul, in the knowledge of what has gone before.

In my work I meet many people who feel that they have either clear or vague memories of other lifetime experiences. When speaking of other lifetimes people are most inclined to say something like, 'I think that I lived another lifetime in Greece/Egypt/Rome or as a nun/monk/farmer/Roman soldier.' But is it the actual 'I' who is living now, in this present incarnation, who was present in those previous lives? Or is it that the 'I' that is living now, has never lived before, although it has access to memories of other 'I's that have lived in other times?

Discarnate teaching – Gildas' perspective

I have already briefly referred in the Introduction to teaching from my discarnate guide, Gildas, about how the organisation of the soul might be seen. The following summary may help you towards a clearer understanding of that organisation.

- There are three main interactive aspects that give higher meaning, purpose, organisation and context to your lives. These are soul, spirit and higher self.
- The soul does not incarnate; it sends out 'beads' of personality (experience gained from a life's journey, as explained in The Thread of Many Lifetimes below). The spirit is present in these beads and it illuminates and vitalises your incarnate being. The soul observes and oversees from the subtle planes.
- The higher self is an aspect of the soul that carries and interprets the growing body of knowledge and wisdom that is acquired by living successive incarnate lives. It organises your pattern of

incarnation and evolution, and decides what kind of incarnation is needed or necessary for the continuation of your eternal learning process.

- When you die, your spirit (otherwise thought of as your essence) returns to the soul so that the learning from the lifetime just ended can be integrated with the learning or experience from other lifetimes.

- When the need for learning through incarnation is over, soul and spirit are totally reunited, as in the chalice of the soul containing the flame of the spirit (see Chapter 1 and Exercise 1, page 7).

The thread of many lifetimes

Gildas has also taught me an understanding of the thread of many lifetimes, as below:

- Your soul is like the thread of a beaded necklace. The beads on the thread are personality beads either waiting to incarnate or who have already been in incarnation and have returned to your soul thread.

- The return of a bead to your soul thread adds knowledge, derived from experience, to the consciousness of your soul and higher self.

- Each incarnation involves a different personality bead. As your soul thread integrates the incarnational experience of each bead it informs beads that have not yet incarnated of the tasks that may need to be undertaken in order to increase or balance past life experience and further your soul's evolution.

- In this way no one bead incarnates more than once, but all beads have access to the memories held by your soul thread. This means that the 'I' that is incarnate at any given time is not an 'I' that has incarnated before. It is an 'I' that can have access to the common memory bank of incarnate experience absorbed by your soul thread and an 'I' that can have pre-set or pre-agreed tasks related to that bank of experience.

Although it is usual, when people speak about past lifetimes, to say, 'When I was a . . .' or 'When I lived in . . .', this can be seen as a kind of shorthand when taken in the context of each bead on your soul thread living a different, separate and one-and-only lifetime. On your quest for deeper understanding of your soul contract and purpose it is important not to over-identify with the experiences of other beads on your soul thread but to consider your life as being in a special context or relationship to them.

The potential burdens of the concepts of 'cause and effect', or 'an eye for an eye and a tooth for a tooth', might lead you to believe that your present life circumstances are directly related to things *you* did wrong and now have to suffer for. Such concepts may also, if everything is going swimmingly, lead into a kind of hubris of believing that *you* must have got it right and that therefore *you* are reaping the benefits and rewards for good behaviour. These can be pitfalls in the path of perfection (Chapter 1, page 1).

Twin souls, soul mates, soul families and group souls

We can use the metaphor of beads on a thread with your soul as a necklace to understand some other concepts that will be referred to later in the book. These are twin souls, soul mates, soul families and group souls. All of these will be referred to in the personal stories that are included as illustrations of how working with your soul manifests into life and consciousness. Below, Gildas' teaching will help you to gain a greater awareness of working with your soul through the relationships of life. Some of these ideas may seem difficult to understand at first, but they are explained further and illustrated through more personal contexts throughout the book. Gildas uses the term 'Source' rather than a more religious and necessarily masculine or paternal term such as 'God'. The Source is Divine, the planner of the universe, the origin of all life. It incorporates masculine and feminine principles equally.

- A human soul is a spark that splits off from the Source and chooses human incarnation as its destiny.
- As it begins the journey of evolution, which, when complete, will lead it back to the Source, the spark partially splits once again.
- The yin, or feminine of its essence, splits from the yang, or masculine (see Glossary).
- These two essences will take different but complementary and interdependent journeys.
- In terms of the image of your soul being like a necklace of beads on a thread, the yin and the yang part are separate strands of the same necklace, joined at the fastening (similar to a double strand of pearls or beads).
- The beads on each strand represent opportunities for incarnation, but the beads from the yin strand will not always be limited to the choice of a female incarnation, just as the beads from the yang strand will not be limited to the choice of a male incarnation. Nevertheless, at the deepest level, personality beads from the yin thread will always carry a stronger yin imprint, and beads from the yang thread will always carry a stronger yang imprint.
- When evolution of the soul is complete, which means that all the beads on each strand of the soul necklace have incarnated and returned, the two strands will become one once more.
- During incarnations before this happens, a bead from one of your soul strands may meet with a bead from its twin strand. This is the meeting that brings about the incarnate experience of meeting with a twin soul or perfect partner.
- Beads from each strand of the necklace of the soul do not always incarnate simultaneously, meaning that a personality bead from your twin soul thread is not necessarily in incarnation at the same time as you are.
- This means that you may not meet with your twin soul, simply because a bead from the other strand is not actually in incarnation for you to meet.
- In your present times, when collective and individual evolution is speeding ahead, the danger is that if twin souls meet in

incarnation, they may be over-absorbed in each other, thus affecting the degree to which each can move forward in the learning process of soul work. When partners are together, their range of experience is similar.

- By electing not to meet with your twin soul in incarnation, each of you separately can cover as much complementary, evolutionary soul work as possible. Part of working with your soul may be the need to accept that the search for your twin soul is not relevant to your present soul contract.

- There are other close and satisfying spiritual family or soul group partnerships that are possible, however. Sometimes too much longing for your true twin soul can lead to undervaluing, or even missing out on, other almost as equally satisfying relationships.

- More than one bead from the same soul strand can be incarnate at any given time. Technically a bead from your own yin or yang soul strand is not a twin soul but a soul mate and when you meet such a bead you may have a very close relationship or friendship.

- Beads from your same soul strand may be your parents or grandparents or your children or grandchildren.

- Beads from your twin soul strand may also be your parents, grandparents, children or grandchildren.

Soul families and soul groups

The structure of your soul is complex. The beads on the double strands of your soul necklace are an integral group or community, but souls also belong to soul families and soul groups. In order to understand this network of souls, Gildas gives some different imagery, and speaks about trees and forests:

- Imagine a tree, then the forest where it stands and then beyond that forest, many other forests of trees.

- The branches on each tree, with leaves, twigs and fruit that spring from each one, are an alternate image for your soul necklace with its beads.

- Leaves, twigs and fruit are the aspects that are put out into incarnation by the branch, which is now the image for your soul thread/higher self.
- The model of the branch on the tree does not adapt so easily to include the concept of twin souls, but the image of branches on a tree illustrates the concept of your soul family.
- Each branch is a soul, and the total tree is your soul family.
- The branches hold a central consciousness for each soul.
- The trunk of the tree holds a joint consciousness for your soul family. The forest of many trees may then be seen as your soul group. (Soul groups and soul families are formed as individual souls evolve. Although the spectrum of issues to be experienced or dealt with may be wide within a soul group – or even within a soul family – all will be involved in supporting each other through the learning process provided by incarnation. Families and groups work together to enable the soul's supreme aim, which is wisdom, to be accomplished. A soul group, or forest of trees, is like an extended family.)
- The forests that are beyond the forest of your particular soul group represent other soul groups. Family souls and soul groups often have a shared incarnate agenda or contract, as indicated above.
- In life you may meet with those who are from the same branch as yourself, those who are from the same tree and those who are from the same forest, as well as those who are from completely different forests.

The start of your soul's journey

With this information to think about, you may also wonder about the start of your soul's journey. The following points will help you to complete the total theoretical picture of your soul's endeavour.

- Souls putting out their first or earliest beads into incarnation are often referred to as 'young souls'. The incarnational planning for these early beads is much more open and free than it is for those that come later, as, at first, there are no karmic causes and effects to be adjusted – no 'as ye sow, so shall ye reap' agendas to be taken into account.

- The early incarnating beads have free rein to start the experiential ball rolling. At this present, here-and-now phase in collective human development, there are very few early, or first-personality beads, from young souls entering or participating in incarnate life. This does not mean that new souls are 'running out', but that because our present times are complex, there are a lot of fresh opportunities for the more experienced souls and so the proportion of new souls to old souls has changed for what is your present time. The balance will be redressed later.

- The main charge for an incarnating early bead from a young soul is to commence exploration of whatever presents itself.

- The young soul can be compared to an explorer wanting to know all earth's unexplored territories and experiences, for the simple reason that they *are* unexplored, or to a mountaineer wanting to climb a mountain simply because it is *there*.

- Once the ball is rolling, as beads return with their experience and learning to the soul thread, there is substance from which further planning can take place.

- As evolution progresses or as your soul conceives of specific tasks it wants to accomplish as well as the balances it wants to achieve or new experiences it wants to add to its 'data base', there will be beads put out into incarnations that have tighter boundaries than before.

- The extreme position on tight boundaries imposed from the soul level can happen during the course of evolution, when, after consultation with the higher self, the next personality bead that is to incarnate is persuaded to hand over almost *all* choice relating to the coming incarnation.

- This means that there is an agreement for the incarnate personality to meet much more limited opportunities during the life span than will an incarnate being who has not made this tight agreement.

Guides and angels

You may also wonder where guides and angels fit into the system of things. The extracts from Gildas' teachings so far refer to the human strand of evolution. Guides belong to this strand. They are beings who have been in incarnation, but are now from evolved souls who will probably not put further personality beads into incarnation. Your personal discarnate guide will belong to your soul group; that is, using the illustration above, from a tree in the same forest as your tree. Each one of us can have access to our own discarnate guide. Whether you are in direct communication with your guide or not, they are helping your soul/higher self to implement and communicate to you the purposes of your incarnation (see also Chapter 9 and Bibliography).

Angels are from a different stream of consciousness than that of the human. They are subtle and diffuse beings of light helping to surround us with Divine light and intelligence. Angels will never be humans, and humans will never be angels. When we are in need, we can, through prayer and invocation, call upon the angelic realms to help and sustain us (see also Chapter 9 and Bibliography).

Before moving on to the greater specifics of working with your soul, the next chapter looks particularly at three aspects or phases of soul work that need to be understood and taken into account as you seek to know your soul work and contract more fully. Soul work comes under three categories: retributive soul work, redemptive soul work and transcendent soul work. The next chapter describes these and helps you to understand their implications for your personal soul work and the way in which you experience your life. This understanding can help you to have a stronger and fuller sense of your involvement with your soul in your present and future planning of your life.

3

Soul Work

Your soul is intent on gaining as many different life experiences as possible. Your present and immediate life is part of a long and rich continuum. Your soul's plans for you are linked to what has gone before; that is, the experience of previously incarnate personality beads from your soul thread. Before incarnation you may have agreed with your soul that you will finish or continue some experience that has already been set in motion or that you will continue to hone certain skills. If previous personality beads have got some aspects of life seriously out of balance, then you may have items in your soul contract or agenda that relate to creating a new balance. If a previous personality bead has gone to some extreme, such as an extreme religious practice or a life of selfishness and hedonism, then you might be asked to explore the opposite. If the opposites have already been explored, then you might be charged with finding a middle way between such extremes.

As well as such designated soul work, your soul will want you to explore the life of your times and to some extent to be an opportunist, taking delight in the very act of living. Evolution is built from all conscious experience and is furthered by free exploration as well as by endeavouring to decode and understand the work your soul particularly wants you to do. It is when life gets tough with obstacles in the way and doors that seem not to open that your soul may want you to focus on one particular aspect of soul work before

you are free to move forward in other ways. Gaining greater awareness of retributive, redemptive and transcendent karma can help you
in knowing the moments in life when it is wise to wait and the
moments when pushing forward is a better strategy. (Karma is where
a personality bead's actions in a previous existence have an effect on
deciding the agenda or contract for the incarnation of another bead
from the same thread.) I hope that the following explanations will
help you to 'read' your soul's intentions more clearly, so that you can
cooperate with them with greater awareness.

Although the notion of 'an eye for an eye and a tooth for a tooth'
is somewhat naive, the experience required by your soul may, nevertheless, include undergoing what it is like to be on the receiving end
of behaviours that have been meted out to others by a previous soul
bead on your soul thread. This statement is not in contradiction to
some of the things already said, because this is not about any kind
of punishment linked personally to you. It is aimed at giving you the
chance to awaken awareness on behalf of your total soul in order to
bring about the balance required. It is a stage of your soul work
sometimes known as the retributive or repentant stage.

Retributive/repentant soul work

This stage of working with your soul is the phase when, in response
to the overview and vision of your higher self, your eternal being
becomes conscious of the necessity to make retribution or repen-
tance for imperfections and imbalances created by a previous
incarnate bead from your soul stem. In the consultation that goes on
before you, as a distinct being, incarnate, you may agree to become
an ambassador for some of this work. Retributive soul work can be
concerned with, or characterised by, extremes or polarities.

Imagine that a previous personality bead from your soul stem has
used power unwisely or 'thrown its weight about'. If this has
happened it could result in a soul contract item for you, in your
present lifetime, of meeting and learning to deal with the kind of
obstacles that make it difficult to feel totally self-empowered. Your

soul would be concerned to support you in managing to work with such obstacles in a way that would bring change and healing to that which had gone previously.

If, in looking at your life (see Exercise 2, page 30 and Exercise 3, page 33) you realise that you have re-presenting issues with power, disempowerment or authority, it would almost certainly mean that working consciously with these issues would be at least a part of your soul work. If you were dealing with an example such as that suggested here, it could be important to make sure that you avoid being a victim of circumstance and so endeavour to manage your present obstacles and challenges in a more inventive way. The following brief personal story may help to make this clearer.

Gloria's story

Gloria had two older brothers and was the only girl born into a family where, even in our present day and age, there was a tradition of rigid male and female roles. Men were the providers and therefore needed to be educated more than women. They expected to work hard, but equally expected to be well looked after by their women-folk. A woman's role was that of having and looking after children, shopping for food, cooking meals and keeping a neat home.

Gloria' mother was content, enjoyed her role as homemaker and did not look for more in life. She had coffee mornings with friends, the family had a holiday every year and her husband honoured her birthday and anniversaries with special treats or outings.

As a child, Gloria loved school and, in particular, learning languages. She wanted to go to university to further her language studies. She was aware of the many interesting jobs that could be open to a competent linguist and wanted to travel. When she outlined her plans to stay on at school and be serious about her studies, she met opposition from both her mother and her father. She was expected to leave school as soon as she was able and find work in a shop or bank, or possibly to do a secretarial course. The message was that she should be looking for no other future than to find a husband, marry and settle down. Until that happened she would be expected to live at home and, when not working, to continue helping her mother as usual.

When Gloria indicated that she did not want to follow this life plan, the opposition to her right to choose her own destiny was powerful. She felt unseen and disempowered but, eventually, of course, when Gloria became an adult, her parents could not control her in the same way. She worked her way through university and fulfilled some of her dreams, but she had to do it all by herself and her life as a student carried extra burdens and responsibilities. Her parents refused to be proud of her and although she continued to keep in touch, she always got the message that she had somehow let everyone down and been selfish.

Gloria came for counselling when she realised that she had an inner battle with every decision she wanted to make in life. She doubted her self-worth and was plagued by a feeling of incompetence and of not being good enough.

Gradually she worked through these feelings and saw exactly what had laid down these patterns in her. She was a counselling client and did not ask for Gildas' help, but my own sense was that part of Gloria's soul contract was about experiencing control and opposition because perhaps another bead on her soul thread had been controlling and powerful over others in a previous lifetime. Gloria could have become a victim of circumstance. She would have been very frustrated if she had not fought for the right to be herself. It was only in finding inner strength and determination that she worked through this retributive soul work and eventually learned to be able to celebrate freely her considerable achievements. At this point, she made the transition into redemptive karma.

A transition

It can be comforting to know that in any given lifetime, your retributive soul work is a transitional stage. It is one that accounts for many of the obstacles, blockages or apparent inequalities that you might observe as occurring right from the start of your life, simply by the circumstances of your birth. The circumstances into which you incarnate are neither 'sentence' nor 'accident' but exist as the result of careful selection. Once you start to realise the significance of the basic 'givens' in your life (see Chapter 4, page 36) it becomes easier to sense the areas in which your retributive soul work may lie and to feel yourself working in true partnership with your soul as you seek transformation and fulfilment. With retributive soul work more fully in your awareness, you will be well on your way, as in Gloria's story, to moving towards the transition into redemptive soul work. Retributive/repentant soul work is partly imposed through the basic circumstances of your birth and initiation into life. As the soul bead incarnating with a contract that relates to what has gone before, you will have taken part in the consultation with your soul/higher self during which the circumstances of your birth and your present incarnation were chosen or decided.

Redemptive soul work

This is the stage where you can actively work to live your life in such a way as to make your heart sing. Any obstacles, blockages and challenges of the retributive stage can be fully accepted, used positively, surmounted or transformed.

Moving into the stage of redemptive soul work is the time where you may begin to feel most aware of working with and for your soul, of having a soul contract and of needing to know more clearly what that contract is about. The transition may be achieved by either circumstantial or attitudinal change, or it might happen with the aid of synchronicity, whereby your soul and the guides and helpers who watch over you will cause you to be in the right place at the right time in your life. In the changeover between redemptive/repentant soul work into the redemptive phase, synchronicity might become a very marked aspect of your life experience.

As Gloria found confidence in herself, even without putting things into the terminology I am using here, she naturally seemed to understand that she had needed to work through opposition in order to find her own right to make decisions about her own life path. In coming for counselling she ensured that she would not get caught up in old patterns or feel guilty about working to fulfil her own personal aims and vision. She later became a translator for an organisation working with refugees and victims of torture. As well as the technical work of translation, Gloria helped others because of her compassion and depth of understanding of their plight, as she too, in a more minor way, had had to fight against being a victim of circumstance. This, as I see it, was her redemptive soul work.

Transcendent soul work

This is more difficult to describe, and there are several synonyms for the words 'transcend' and 'transcendent', but I think that in terms of explaining or understanding your transcendent soul work the most useful synonyms are 'surpassing', 'exceeding', 'going beyond' and 'rising above'.

In the phase of retributive soul work your soul aims to make you conscious of causes that have been set in motion by other soul beads in previous incarnations. These directly affect your present life, as you will have taken on the task of finding some kind of resolution. In the phase of redemptive soul work you make either circumstantial or attitudinal change to bring about this resolution or balance.

In the phase of transcendent soul work, however, you tend to surpass yourself and succeed beyond your expectations. At the retributive and redemptive stages you may experience a certain bondage to the original cause and effect. At the transcendent stage your experience of bondage is over, the balance has been made, the lesson assimilated and your way forward becomes clear and uninhibited by obstacles. Transcendent soul work is a stage of full awareness of communication and cooperation with your soul and its purposes for your present lifetime. Stuart's experience is an illustration of this.

Stuart's story

Stuart seemed to have lurched from crisis point to crisis point for most of his life. When I met him, he was an inspirational speaker at a spiritual conference and his own story illustrated (though not using the same words) each of the stages of soul work (retributive, redemptive and transcendent). An only child, with a reasonably happy early childhood, Stuart was eight years old when his parents went through a bitter divorce. For many years afterwards he seemed unable to make sense of life. Even his early friendships were marred by childhood jealousies, competitiveness and a certain amount of victimisation. He was intellectually able, but had no motivation for study. He left school as soon as possible and tried to find a purpose in such things as working with animals and gardening, but could not sustain any sense of continuity. He eventually mixed in with a group of people who lived in a squat in a town centre and spent their time sleeping, lounging and listening to music. Although there was no serious drug problem in the group they all smoked cannabis and had dropped out from the normal patterns of life and society.

To get money, Stuart had to go through the benefit system, and there were regular interviews asking how many jobs he had applied for recently and demanding that he apply for others. One day his attitude changed; he did not know exactly what had 'woken him up' but felt it was a definite 'call' from his soul. After one of the benefit interviews he suddenly had a deep insight into how he was missing out on life and how, in the existence he had been living, he had been under an illusion. He realised that he was fit and well and was an unnecessary drain on society when he could be active in some way. He decided to do some voluntary work with emotionally disturbed young people. He got himself fit and gradually discovered skills as an inspirational team leader. He went on to train for outward bound work and at last felt fulfilled in life.

Stuart also became interested in the meaning of life and read widely and deeply about spirituality and spiritual practice. He was drawn to self-discovery groups and explored his inner depths. One day, he became inspired by the thought of working not only with outward bound work but also with 'inward bound' work, so that as well as helping young people to gain courage and self-value in tackling outer challenges, he could help them to discover their inner gifts and talents, their vision and imagination. He became a pioneer in such work and, as it became successful, he realised that he had transcended all his own depression and lack of motivation and found a quality of life that went to fulfilment and beyond. At this point, in my view, he had entered the transcendent phase of soul work.

How the three phases work together

To some extent these three phases or stages of soul work are linear and hierarchical in sequence, yet they also co-exist or operate alongside each other, especially at the retributive and redemptive stages. The ground rules of life are intricate. You usually have more than one piece of soul work to accomplish in any given incarnation. At any particular moment, then, you may have some life issues at the retributive stage, some at the redemptive stage and others at the transcendent.

At this stage, Michael's story or case history may also serve to help some of the theoretical framework to come alive for you. The case histories given in this book are sometimes those of people who have come to Gildas for spiritual advice or counsel and sometimes from clients of mine who have come to me for a course of psychotherapy or counselling.

Michael's story is one of moving from his retributive/repentant soul work to the redemptive phase.

Michael's story
Aged 35 years, Michael came for a channelling session with Gildas. His main reason for coming, he said, was because all his life, he had felt as though he was running against the tide. He had tried hard, worked hard, and endeavoured to find creative solutions to life's dilemmas but he felt as though life had never really taken off for him or treated him kindly. He craved success but it always remained

elusive. He felt himself to be a good potential leader, but in every job he did he was never 'top man', only the assistant or second in command. He felt frustrated and unseen.

Michael was the second of three sons and had suffered badly from what is sometimes called 'middle child' syndrome: he was not special by virtue of being either the eldest or the youngest. Everything he did, his older brother had done before. It then seemed to Michael that his younger brother came along and did all the things that Michael had tried to do, but much better and at an earlier age.

After getting a second-class degree in psychology, Michael had made his career in personnel work. He was very interested in staff training and team leadership. He had assisted in the training of many a team leader but somehow never managed to become one himself. On one occasion, just as he became due for routine promotion, the firm he was working for was about to change location.

Although the offer was there for him to relocate, Michael had decided that it was too much of an upheaval to move from one end of the country to the other. His decision was partly made because he wanted to sustain his relationship with his current girlfriend, which seemed to be going well. Previously, relationships had been just one of the many things that never quite took off in Michael's life. However, just as the firm moved and Michael had foregone his promotion, his girlfriend decided that she was not ready to make a commitment and settle down. She wanted to travel the world.

For Michael it seemed as though this was the final straw to break the camel's back. About a year earlier, trying every way he knew to make sense of what he saw as his life's burden, Michael had read some books recommended by a friend that opened up his spiritual interests. The friend then made the suggestion that, as Michael was at a crisis point in his life, he should seek guidance from another perspective or dimension. Michael was recommended to come for a channelling session with Gildas.

As he spoke with Gildas, it was obvious that Michael was very set on bringing about definite circumstantial change. He was not easily going to become either contented or fulfilled by attitudinal change.

He wanted to know if there was any way that he could bring about changes in his personal power and success. He was desperate to do something that made him feel he was ahead and not just a worker at the 'coal face'.

Gildas gave Michael hope, although he also suggested that one way of feeling more contented might be to change his paradigms of success by positively re-evaluating some of the events of his life and revising his ideas about what constitutes success. In this way he could increase his sense of self-esteem and become a kinder observer of himself.

Gildas spoke to Michael about retributive soul work and how its challenges could lead to a more conscious understanding of major soul tasks. Although Michael had been feeling very frustrated, Gildas pointed out that it is often the thing that you find most difficult to deal with that is a major soul task, if not *the* major soul task. Once this is known and accepted, then a determination to resolve the dilemmas that frustrate you can be renewed. Should they remain intransigent, knowing that you are working, nevertheless, at what the soul wants you to work at, can completely change your perception of life's ups and downs. You can move from feeling that life is against you and halt the well-known psychological process of affirming and re-affirming negative self-fulfilling prophecies about your self-worth. Michael in particular, could move into a sense of knowing that as long as his soul task was being addressed to the best of his ability there really was no shame in not being seen to be top man.

Gildas also said that around the incarnate age of 35 years (Michael's age) is often the time when a seemingly intractable retributive soul task will suddenly change. This transition may be made by a sudden breakthrough (in some cases even a breakdown, see Chapter 8, page 125) or an unexpected but synchronous event (see Glossary for further notes on synchronicity).

The main reason that Michael wanted to be a success, Gildas suggested, was not really about image or being seen to be able to do it. He felt that Michael was carrying an imprint from the life of another personality bead from his soul stem who had used power in order to control or to trample on others. Michael, therefore, had a soul contract that gave him an inner burning and overriding desire to show that power could be held and used, not for its own sake, but with wisdom and selflessness to enable others. Finding it difficult to attain this power and put it into practice was a way of making him more conscious of the task for which he was an ambassador.

Finding greater understanding

In transpersonal psychology, when sudden insights come, or are affirmed during counselling or consultation they are often described as 'Ahaaa!' moments. On this occasion, when Gildas had finished speaking, Michael said that he had felt several of these moments while listening.

Although Gildas only highlighted, without going into details, the theme of the life where a previous incarnate bead had misused power, Michael felt relieved to have had it mentioned. He had partly thought that his drive to power was about one-upmanship or to please his parents and had therefore secretly labelled himself as 'shallow'. Yet, underneath he had also always felt or hoped that it was more than that.

For Michael, having it affirmed that he *needed* power or advancement in his work and life in order to fulfil a redemptive task for his soul, rather than only to enhance his own self-esteem or street cred was already making him feel more 'connected' and of greater depth and substance. Realising that he was striving to work with his soul and achieve a balance at a much higher and wider level opened up a whole new perspective for him.

In some ways, it might be said that this whole new angle that Michael was gradually assimilating and feeling very relieved about, *was* attitudinal change. In other ways Michael was experiencing a deep understanding of his soul task and the source of his drive. In so doing he was shedding his perception of himself as a victim of circumstance or a 'loser' who couldn't accept loss with dignity. It was actually very moving to see that his paradigms of success were changing, there and then, moment by moment, in the session.

He felt that now, with a greater understanding of his soul work, that success lay in the process of addressing his task rather than in actually realising power and proving himself through it. His whole body posture seemed to change. He understood that there was a lot to work on and a whole new perspective to be learned and considered. He said that he would think about returning either for some therapy sessions or for further consultation with Gildas when he had thought about it more.

In the event, a few weeks later, Michael telephoned me, not to book another appointment but to tell me that he had applied for, and obtained, the kind of post he had long been hoping for. He felt that his success in doing so might have been partly due to his transition from retributive to redemptive soul work having been due anyway, but also attributed it to relaxing his need to prove himself. He had not been overanxious, blatantly status seeking, over-competitive or pompous in his interview, as he now realised he had previously tended to be. He felt he had shown himself to be quietly confident, competent and experienced enough to do work he really wanted to do and had been able to convey this to the interviewing panel. He said that he would always hold in mind that he was now working much more consciously with, and for, his soul and felt sure that he would have a much clearer understanding of its language and signals and more direct access to its guidance in future.

Exercises on reflecting

The following exercises are designed to help you to reflect more deeply and personally on some of the issues raised in this chapter and to prepare you for the work in the following chapters.

These exercises – Meditative Life Review and Mental Life Review – are a linked pair and should be taken together, or as soon after each other as possible. Before you begin, read through Preparing for the Exercises on page 5.

Exercise 2: *meditative life review*

You will need your special notebook, or some easily accessible
sheets of paper and some crayons or pastels, as at each stage of
the following meditative exercise there is an opportunity to use
meditative drawing. This exercise is meditative and heart
centred. Rather than using your mind to think things out, just
try to stay open to images and memories that come sponta-
neously, without forcing them or judging them in any way. The
drawing interludes are also designed to be a continuation of the
meditative mode. Some people like to use their non-dominant
hand for such drawing, as this can help in keeping the mode
meditative, open and creative.

1. Make sure that you will be comfortable and undisturbed.
   Find your comfortable position.

2. Focus on the rhythm of your breathing. Be aware of each
   in-breath and out-breath, not trying to alter its tempo in
   any specific way, but allowing it to find its natural flow.

3. Sense your breath as coming in and out at the 'petals' of
   your heart centre or chakra (life energy centre). This lies in
   the centre of your body and aura on the same level as your
   physical heart (see Glossary).

4. As your regular breathing helps your heart chakra to open,
   get a sense of entering your own inner space or dimension.

5. Endeavour to find a meditative sense of the moment of
   your birth in this present lifetime. Focus on a feeling, an
   image, energy or a colour rather than on any factual details.

6. After a few moments, retaining your meditative mode and

continuing to use the heart breathing for focusing and refocusing into it, take your paper and colours, and move into intuitive or meditative drawing mode, letting the image, energy or colour your have already sensed develop more as you do so.

7. Keeping your heart breath regular, and maintaining the vision of what you have drawn, put the paper and colours aside and refocus into your inner space or dimension.

8. Without trying to remember specific events, ask to be taken to an image, energy, feeling or colour associated with an important time in your early childhood.

9. Keeping your meditative mode as before, use the paper to draw meditatively again.

10. Keeping your heart breath regular, and maintaining the vision of what you have drawn, put the paper and colours aside and refocus into your inner space or dimension.

11. Without trying to remember specific events, ask to be taken to an image, energy, feeling or colour associated with an important time in your late childhood or early teen years.

12. Keeping your meditative mode as before, use the paper to draw meditatively again.

13. Keeping your heart breath regular, and maintaining the vision of what you have drawn, put the paper and colours aside and refocus into your inner space or dimension.

14. Without trying to remember specific events, ask to be taken to an image, energy, feeling or colour associated with an important time in your early adulthood.

15. Keeping your meditative mode as before draw meditatively again.

16. Keeping your heart breath regular, and maintaining the vision of what you have drawn, put the paper and colours aside and refocus into your inner space or dimension.

17. Without trying to remember specific events, ask to be taken to an image, energy, feeling or colour associated with one or more important times between your early adulthood and the age you are now.

18. Keeping your meditative mode as before, draw meditatively once more.

19. Begin to come out of your deeper meditative mode, but keep a sense of stillness and quietness around you, as you now consider the drawings you have made. If they are associated to memorable happenings, write a few words beside each one to help you to register that memory.

20. Keeping within your sense of stillness, look now at what you have drawn and anything you have written and try to recall the feeling quality associated with the times that you have brought to mind during this meditative and reflective journey.

21. Remain centred in this further contemplation for not more than 20 minutes.

22. Gradually return to your awareness of your breath in your heart centre or chakra.

23. Return to a full awareness of your whole physical body and

particularly to your connection with the ground.

24. Visualise a cloak of light with a hood right around you.

25. Become aware of your surroundings and slowly come back to normal everyday consciousness.

Exercise 3: *mental life review*

This exercise is designed to be taken after Exercise 2. You will need your notebook or some sheets of paper and a pen or pencil. Before you begin, read through Preparing for the Exercises on page 5.

This exercise is designed as a thinking, or cognitive, exercise, using your head rather than your heart. Similar to Exercise 2 above, it is a review of your life. There are some suggested headings, which are intended to make you think about your life memories and how you might group them under each one. You may need to spend more than one session with this exercise, and indeed the two exercises together form a basis that you will need to refer to again and again as you work through this book and seek to be able to decode your soul work or soul contract.

1. Making sure that you will be undisturbed, and using your notebook or paper for jotting things down as you go, consider any life events you would group under the following headings:
   a. Symbolic 'knocks on the head' – times when you feel you have been 'knocked back' or brought up short, because of circumstances or obstacles in your life
   b. Symbolic 'kicks from behind' – times when something has spurred you on, or seemingly propelled or moved you forward unexpectedly.

c. Things that seem to get re-presented in your life – these might be opportunities to shine, or times when it has not been possible to follow a vision or plan because of a similar obstacle presenting itself.

d. Given relationships – as with your family of origin and perhaps your extended family. What were, and are, they like? What was/is their quality? What did/do they give you (that you appreciate or that you felt uncomfortable with)? What did they not give you that you might have wanted? What did they teach you?

e. Relationships you made in general – at school, college, at work, in general. Which were special? Which were difficult? Which were helpful? Which were close? Do you keep lasting relationships? Include your love life or partnerships here.

f. Illnesses you have had or still have.

g. Physical strengths or weaknesses.

h. Doors that have seemed closed to you.

i. Losses and deprivations.

j. Blockages and obstacles.

2. You will probably find some overlap in these headings, but use the ones that give you food for thought and don't worry if you note down the same experience under more than one heading.

3. As with the first exercise, when you have finished reflecting on the different headings, take some time to consider the notes you have made.

4. As soon as you can, take an opportunity to compare your meditative, heart-centred images from Exercise 2 with your more mental reflections from Exercise 3. Feel into how the images and drawings from Exercise 2 relate to, or give a

different dimension to, the more mental and factual process of Exercise 3.

The process that you have been through in these two linked exercises will continue to work on in your thoughts, feelings and insights. If you are keeping a special notebook or journal you can continue to add thoughts, reflections or memories, written or drawn, as you continue your process of endeavouring to understand your soul contract and how to work more actively and consciously with it.

The reflections you have made in these two exercises will help you to refer everything to your own personal process as you read and assimilate the next chapters. In Chapter 4 I move on to the process of decoding items of your soul contract from the basic givens of your life.

4

Decoding Your Soul Purpose

Your soul has an agenda for your life and you have made a contract with your soul. All too often, once you are in incarnation, the exact nature of both the agenda and the contract can be difficult to read. Part of your soul's determination to make you conscious means that you are, therefore, challenged to break your soul's code in order to gain the determination and awareness that makes you an effective ambassador for the evolutionary purposes of your soul.

How do I know what my soul contract is?

A common and frequently repeated question relating to soul contracts is: 'If there are things my soul wants me to do in this present lifetime and a contract has been made, why isn't there some efficient system of letting me know what those things are and what the contract is?'

There is no definitive answer to this question but the following conversation between two characters in the book *Labyrinth* by Kate Mosse perhaps attempts that answer:

'Tell me' ... he said, turning to face her, 'Do you believe in destiny? Or is it the path we choose to follow that makes us who we are?

'I —' she started, then stopped. She was no longer sure what she thought ...

'Do you believe that you can change your destiny?' he said, seeking an answer. Alice found herself nodding, 'Otherwise, what's the point? If we are simply walking a path preordained, then all the experiences that make us who we are – love, grief, joy, learning, changing – would count for nothing.'

Indeed, if you *were* to be born with a proscribed and known list of categorical tasks to be accomplished then life would consist only of that. You might tick them off when done to the best of your ability, but when they were completed all that would be left would be to prepare for death. Such an existence would be over-regulated, without access to spontaneity or the joy of developing your individuality and creative awareness.

The circumstances of your birth

As you will certainly not have been born clutching a definitive soul contract or letter from your soul listing the tasks to be accomplished in your present lifetime, where do you begin the search to understand your soul-contract clues? The initially most fertile place is to consider, in some depth, the circumstances of your birth. Where you find yourself at the beginning of your life has fallen into place according to your soul's plan, not just as a chance occurrence.

The basic outline of your soul contract

When you, a soul bead, die at the end of your incarnation, you return to your soul thread or necklace, as explained in Chapter 2. The experience gained during the life you have lived is thus added to the total experience and knowledge of your soul thread.

Everything that has happened to each soul bead is registered and considered. It is not assessed in a judgemental way, but your higher self makes a note of new experiences that have been explored, balances that have been achieved, imbalances that have been set in motion and opportunities that may not have been followed through. It appraises the status quo. Out of this evaluation comes the outline plan or soul contract for the next personality bead preparing to incarnate.

The personality bead that is due for incarnation is, at this stage, privy to much of this assessment and planning, although during the process of being conceived, gestated and born, most of it is wiped from the personality's awareness. This is one of the mysteries of incarnation and soul work. In many incarnations the personality may be unaware of any concept of soul and so will work 'blind'. As soon as you take on an incarnation where you develop a more philosophical or spiritual approach to living and understanding life, however, you can aspire, and learn how, to work more consciously with your soul as explained in this book.

Soul purpose and choice are therefore fully present from before your conception, through your birth and throughout your incarnate life. With the realisation that all has been carefully planned and nothing has happened by chance, it becomes more possible to decipher, and therefore to cooperate with, your soul's intentions. All the basic tools for the things that your soul wants you, as the present incarnate personality bead, to learn and to do, are there.

The 'givens' of life

The main choices decided together by you, as the incarnating personality and your soul, are what I call the 'givens' of life. These set the peripheral boundaries which, as we have seen, for a young soul will be quite flexible, but for a more evolved soul may be tighter, binding the incarnate personality to less choice.

These 'givens' need to be considered and recognised before moving on to look at the kind of obstacles, challenges and opportunities that give your soul more control over the direction of your life, but which also offer occasion for creative compromise and for learning how to be at one with your soul contract even when the life journey seems very difficult indeed.

The 'givens' that have been laid down are set and unalterable.

Many of them will affect the available spectrum of choice for you, as a conscious, incarnate personality, for the duration of your life.

The crossroads and turning points

Your soul/higher self suggests these initial, life-framework choices to you, the incarnating personality, as a basis that will provide you with the soul work that will bring the optimum evolutionary chances for all aspects concerned. These choices will include challenge and limitation as well as opportunity. Although everything has been laid down and nothing happens by chance, there may seem something of a paradox in that this does not mean that you have a totally binding destiny. Within the framework of the selections that have been made for your life, you will still encounter crossroads and turning points where genuine personal or individual choice is either available or required. The selections made by your soul or the 'givens' of your life give you a framework or periphery beyond which it is difficult to step, but within that periphery there is still a great deal of choice and route planning in which you can, and need to be, fully and freely active.

Becoming increasingly aware of how your soul 'thinks' and being able to put your present life into a wider context enables you to work more consciously with, and for, your soul. So, it is time to look at what these chosen factors are, which give your life a certain circumscription.

The basic 'givens'

Your parents are chosen. The geographical area, historical time and culture for your incarnation are chosen. Your initial social milieu is chosen. At the interactive level between souls, your parents will have agreed to invite you to incarnate as their child and you will have agreed to do so. Your soul together with your siblings' souls may also have made evolutionarily reasoned choices to be born to the same parents and into the same family. These are the selections that are made before your physical conception takes place and which include, perhaps most unalterably, your gender, body type, emotional constitution and mental orientation. Even the moment of your birth is chosen, so that you are born under the influence of those astrological constellations that will help to shape your opportunities, challenges and responses to life.

Choice of gender

As has been seen, one of the chosen 'givens' for your present incarnation is that of gender. Except in special circumstances, this choice is unalterable. At a simple, obvious and eminently readable level, it can be implied that this decision has been made according to whether your soul needs to add more masculine lives or more feminine lives to its total experience, but although the obvious and the simple are important, when you read more deeply most of the soul's choices are also more intricate.

Your soul's choice of gender is almost certain to be linked to wider or more complex soul issues than ensuring a balanced number of masculine and feminine lives. Historical time, racial and cultural tradition as well as geographical location will all have a bearing on the lessons and challenges you will face in the gender that your soul has chosen.

As a male or female you not only have a differently functioning body which influences your basic role in life, you also have to deal with any cultural, or perhaps religious, expectations associated with gender roles. In our present Western culture there is great emphasis on equality of opportunity, particularly between men and women. Those of us who have chosen to incarnate at this time into this culture have chosen to be part of all the complexities and struggles that this aspect of collective or racial evolution can present. Incarnating at this time to have the experiences and challenges thus offered may well be an important, but less immediately obvious, item on your soul agenda.

Choice of parents

Your choice of parents determines your genetic patterning and biochemistry. All of these, irrespective of whether you are male or female, have much to do with shaping your body type, your gifts, aptitudes, your emotional and your mental constitution. In turn, these aspects are also influenced by environment and nurture. These latter circumstances are another evidence of the attention to detail that your soul's planning has and are intricately connected to your soul's choice of parents, historical time of incarnation, geographical location and culture.

Genetic and soul families

Although the choosing of parents is important for your genetic patterning and biochemistry, parents and siblings are also chosen on the basis of closeness at a soul level. If you have chosen to be born into a family where there is little or no soul connection, then you may, as Julia did (See Julia's story, page 46), feel as though you somehow don't belong, or that you are of a different substance. To choose your family of origin mainly on the basis of genetic inheritance can be a challenging emotional experience. If your family of origin are also close at a soul level, then, unless some of your family are playing a confronting teaching role for you (see Chapter 5) you will feel more at home and in the company of like-minded people who fully support your incarnational journey.

Genetic inheritance, gifts and aptitudes

Your body is your genetic inheritance from your parents and ancestors. A great deal in your life may depend upon what type of body you have. If you are well co-ordinated or athletic, then you are likely to be interested and proficient in sports of all kinds, such as mountaineering, dance, team sports, riding, driving, swimming, athletics and many more.

With natural ability and inclination in any given area, you will probably be encouraged to develop what you have and put it to good use. In the areas where you are gifted you may be offered opportunities less easily available to others. Your physical or other aptitudes thus become an important ingredient in how your life is shaped.

Its significance in the plan of your soul

Your soul may have arranged for you to have these attributes in order to help to ensure that your life goes in a certain direction designed to take in the kind of experiences it desires for its continuing evolutionary programme.

If you have abilities and they are encouraged, at least one area of life and evolution may be straightforward, satisfying and simple. Yet there are all kinds of complexities that can arise from almost every 'given'. With natural giftedness it may all be well and good if you have been born into a family that values what you have and is prepared to be supportive and take it seriously. It is a very different story if you receive opposition instead of support.

Most of us will be familiar with the inspirational and moving story of the gifted dancer Billy Elliot who, in spite of financial hardship and a father who was initially against his son dancing, was able to be trained at the Royal Ballet. In this, there is a happy ending, and many lessons learned for all concerned, but it is a poignant story, illustrating the way in which life can present some of the more complex opportunities for working with your soul. The case histories, or stories, related in each chapter of this book, will help you to see more of the twists, turns and intricacies that lift seemingly obvious basic choices into the realms of more active work with, and recognition of, your soul's intentions.

Nature or nurture?

You come into incarnation then, with your unique combination of physical, mental, emotional and spiritual attributes. Biologists, philosophers, psychologists and clergy all study human nature. All take part in the continuing debate about, and research into, whether it is nature or nurture that determines our individuality. The soul definitely uses both, closely associated with your choice of parents and culture, geographical location and historical time of incarnation, as it lays down that framework for your soul contract beyond which it is extremely difficult to stray.

Like Billy Elliott, you may have obvious special talents or passions that influence the way in which you unfold or wish to unfold. Are you drawn to the world of art, invention, mathematics, teaching, medicine, nursing, healing, social work, music, acting, dance, sport, politics or leadership? These are but a few of the possibilities for generations in the Western world today.

Even as recently as 150 years ago, whatever your aptitudes, the breadth and potential of choice would have been greatly limited. This is another illustration of the difference the historical time of incarnation can make. Perhaps when the spectrum was limited by the way in which life, travel and communications worked, your soul had an easier task of making sure that, in each incarnation, you were optimally placed in life, for all that it wanted you to learn

Themes that challenge

Beyond giftedness or aptitudes are the underlying themes that challenge or attract you as you grow and develop. Family and culture often have a deep influence on what these might be. In considering them you will find the broader aspects or clauses within your soul contract revealing themselves gradually and progressively from the ground of your basic 'givens'. When you give your attention to these things and name and define them, you will see clearer information about your soul contract and increasing opportunities for creative interpretation of, and cooperation with, its clauses.

Among the themes to identify are: power; love; relationships; wealth; poverty; body; sexuality; religion and belief; control; health; social position; possessions; fears; feeling displaced; image; acceptance; rejection; expectation; wounding; victimhood; dilemmas of action and inaction; choice; authority; and the search for approval. This is not a total or exhaustive list, and more than one theme may be in play in any given lifetime and be in progress in a different phase of soul work (retributive, redemptive or transcendent – see Chapter 3).

Groups and series of lives

Your soul's choice of 'givens', for any particular lifetime, will, at the more complex level of interaction, light the fuses or provide the stimulation required to set the next phase of work on any given theme in motion.

The several or many lifetimes that are lived by the beads from your soul thread fall into groups or series, in which work on specific themes is developed. These groups or series of lives do not necessarily follow each other linearly, systematically or hierarchically. In some lives it can be that you are working with several different issues as though 'rounding off' more than one series. Your life 'givens', when considered carefully and symbolically, can help in obtaining more understanding of even the most complex soul contracts.

A personal story
From birth, although it was not actually part of my genetic inheritance, I had what was thought to be a 'lazy eye'. For the early part of my childhood, the Second World War was still in progress and even when it ended, resources and the availability and expertise of medical help were not as they are now. Although various attempts were made to help my eyes to work in unison, it was not until I was 12 years old that it was discovered that my right eye is not 'lazy' but very partially sighted, maybe due to a birth injury. As I learned more about symbolism from my study of transpersonal psychology, I realised that the right eye is connected to looking outwardly, whereas the left eye is connected to looking inwardly and to having a vivid inner life. I also realised that more perfectly balanced eyesight would have made me very keen on sport of all kinds. My activities

in general have not been hampered by my eyesight problem, but my hand-eye coordination *is* affected and so the sporting life was not an option for me, making it clearer that I needed to concentrate on developing other gifts and aptitudes.

In my dreams and from some past-life recall, I experience myself as full of physical prowess. My conclusion is that other personality beads from my soul stem have thoroughly explored those life options and experiences and that among my 'givens' for this present lifetime had to be something that would stop me from repeating or chasing accomplishments that are not presently required as part of my soul's evolution.

There is a saying of Native American origin, that states, 'Nothing exists except in relationship to something else.' Remembering the truth and wisdom in this statement can help in realising that in terms of evolution and soul relationship nothing currently presenting in your life stands in isolation from what has gone before. Looking at what is given to you in your present lifetime and imaginatively understanding what might have gone before, helps you to open up the channels for insight into the themes and even the details of the stories of the personality beads from your soul stem that have gone before. Most of the items in your present soul contract will exist only in relationship to something else that has either gone before, co-exists in the moment, or is leading into the future.

Soul councils

Your incarnation to specific parents is chosen, not by your own higher self or soul in isolation, but by something like a 'council' of interacting higher selves. Such a council will also have planned your potential meetings with many 'significant others' in your life. Pre-incarnational agreements between souls mean that you will have the opportunity to meet those who will help to give your incarnation meaning, those with whom you sense a special spiritual bond as well as those who will teach and challenge you to learn the lessons and have the experiences that both your, and their, souls desire as part of a joint life intention.

Synchronicity: the master tool of your soul

The ways in which your soul seeks to ensure that you meet the right person at the right time can be fascinating and are often attributed to that mysterious ingredient in life known as synchronicity. Although most guides, because they are no longer bound by the time dimension that is so much part of incarnation, will tell you that they find it difficult to answer any questions posed to them that begin with 'When?' Nevertheless, together with your soul, your guides are involved in the timing of important life moments. Synchronicity is not only a matter of chance events and is more than its oft-quoted definition of 'meaningful coincidence'. It is evidence of the careful work of the master planning department of your soul together with its advisors and helpers (see also Chapter 9).

The whole way in which your life 'givens' form a firm foundation for the work your soul is offering you for your present incarnation is an example of astonishing, minute and synchronous attention to detail. Chapter 5 considers our teachers in life and relationships of all kinds. Meanwhile, Julia's story, below, serves as something of an illustration of the difference between soul and genetic families and leads on to the subject matter of Chapter 5.

Julia's story
Aged 35 years, Julia came for therapy because for most of her life she had sensed herself as a misfit. She felt that she could not get anything right in life, particularly in the field of relationships. Unlike Michael (page 25), Julia was not concerned with having her abilities recognised and fulfilling them. She was desperately searching for a sense of belonging. She wondered if there could be something intrinsically wrong with her. Despite having a job that she loved and a salary that enabled her to have her own flat and car,

she said, 'I just don't feel comfortable in my own skin, I feel like a square peg in a round hole.'

When I asked about her childhood she said that she had been well-nurtured with no notable deprivations, except a deep sense of not being in harmony with, or even of the same substance as, her older sister, her parents and even with either her maternal or paternal grandparents.

When she was eight, Julia learned about how children might be adopted if their natural parents could not look after them properly. She suddenly felt a great sense of relief. Even at that early age she felt a dilemma had been resolved. She became sure that it would turn out to be not only that she *felt* as though she didn't belong but that she *actually* didn't. Her subsequent questioning of her parents, with her declaration that she didn't mind that she was adopted and was grateful for all that had been done for her but just needed to be told the truth, had, understandably, not gone down well. Her parents' somewhat shocked reassurances that Julia truly was their flesh and blood had left her even more puzzled. It seemed that a gateway of explanation had opened, only to slam shut again.

When I suggested that, from a spiritual point of view, children can be born into genetic, rather than soul families and that this can bring about all the feelings of not belonging or finding a proper niche and the right companionship in life, I could see a sense of relief spread across her face and relaxation in her body.

Julia gradually realised that if she stopped comparing herself with her family of origin's patterns and paradigms of success and happiness, in the hope of finding the same for herself, she could let go of pressure and tension. Her parents and sister were very conventional in what they required to make them happy. Heather, Julia's sister, had happily gone to work in a bank, married a work colleague and now had two children. She and her husband lived within easy reach of both sets of parents, who also got on well together. Much social life revolved around family gatherings for birthdays and anniversaries, with both sets of grandparents doting on the grandchildren. When Julia attended such gatherings she felt, she said, 'like a spare part'. She couldn't get it right. If she didn't attend she was criticised, if she did she felt under duress to do what her sister had done, which in the view of the family was what 'getting a life together' was all about.

Julia had trained in horticulture and was considering setting up her own business. She needed a lot of physical stamina for the work she did, and although she had some social life with colleagues, she had no really deep friendships. To some extent her family admired what Julia had achieved but she felt that they did not really understand or value her ambition and way of life, and she yearned for their approval. She felt that she would like to travel or even live abroad, but had somehow got herself into a mindset where, in over-anxiously considering what her family would think, she was constantly denying herself permission to branch out as *she* truly longed to do. In order to find a sense of belonging at a family level, she was making unacceptable compromises, and, apart from the satisfaction of her working days, was feeling socially more and more inadequate with a diminishing quality of life.

In talking it through over a number of weeks, Julia gradually began to realise that there was nothing intrinsically wrong with *her*. The world she was turning to for approval and desperately trying to fit into was actually not in tune with her true and personal reality or nature. She was so focused on trying to get a sense of belonging at the family level that she had not considered that *difference* from those who had born and nurtured her was not *wrong*. The idea of genetic and spiritual families being two different things was very new to her and she had not, therefore, taken into account that she might find people outside the tight circle of her family of origin who could give her the sense of family she so desperately craved. This meant that she had not focused enough energy into finding friends and companionship beyond her genetic kith and kin. *She* was not wrong, but had been looking over-intensely in the wrong *direction* for a resolution to her deeply felt dilemma.

Julia had socially-inherited paradigms to change and expectations of herself to modify. She had to develop self-confidence and to learn how to look at life through a wider-angled lens. Such changes, which eventually enabled her to move on, did not come quickly or necessarily easily, but come they did. She eventually moved to Spain to work in a horticultural project there. She used the opportunity and challenge to join a completely different circle of people and put more energy into friendships. She began, at last, to feel a sense of belonging.

She still came home for some family celebrations, but because she felt confident in her own way of life and had stopped apologising for it, she was able to enjoy them more. She also felt that in her new acceptance of herself and her need to go her own way, her family subtly felt more comfortable with, and therefore more accepting of, her. They even expressed interest and excitement in her ability to live abroad, and the last I heard there was a plan for all the family to spend a holiday, near Julia, in Spain.

Julia had not come for specific spiritual or soul help. Her learning about her soul task or contract was implicit rather than explicit. During her therapy, she did, however, realise that she had her genetic inheritance to thank for her body, which was strong and full of stamina, and had therefore enabled her to do hard physical work. She also realised, eventually, that being born into circumstances where she had felt so little sense of kinship had opened up possibilities for her exploration of life and friendships rather than narrowing it. She had needed to view, take on, and adapt to a different perspective in order to set herself free.

Exercise on looking at your 'givens'

The following exercise leads on from Exercises 2 and 3 from Chapter 3. It is designed to help you to look more closely at the 'givens' your soul decreed or decided upon as you were born into this present lifetime, and to begin to write down your soul contract as it might be interpreted from these.

Exercise 4: *endeavouring to specify and write down some items of my soul contract*

You will need your special notebook, if you have begun to keep one, or some sheets of paper so that you can make notes. This is an informal reflective exercise and is not designed to be contained within a certain time space. If you think about this regularly, even at the back of your mind, over a period of days or weeks, it will help you to get more deeply into reading the possible messages from your soul that are encapsulated in the events of your life.

Before you begin, read through Preparing for the Exercises on page 5. This does not mean that every insight will come from the more formal sessions or approach. As you get further into this work, you will probably find that related ideas and insights will 'pop up' as you go about the routine tasks of your life.

1. Refer back to your meditative drawings from Exercise 2 and to your mental reflections from Exercise 3.

2. Particularly focus again on your family of origin and the circumstances of your birth, under the headings:
   a. Time of incarnation.
   b. Geographical place of incarnation.
   c. Race.
   d. Social milieu.
   e. Gender. What it may have meant to your parents and family circumstances. What it has meant to you.

3. Reflect on these headings from this and the previous chapter, if necessary reading again the points and information given under each one:
   a. Soul or genetic families (page 41 and Julia's story, page 46).

b. Genetic inheritance, gifts and aptitudes and their significance in the plan of your soul (page 41).

c. Themes that challenge (page 43).

d. Synchronicity: the master tool of your soul (page 46).

e. The basic outline of your soul contract (page 37).

f. Crossroads and turning points (page 39)

Keep reflecting on these points and themes, over a number of days or even weeks. When you feel that you are very familiar with them and have made additional notes to those you made in Exercise 2 of any insights, thoughts and feelings you are having as you read and re-read, on a new page in your notebook or clean sheet of paper write the heading:

My Soul Purpose or Contract for This Present Lifetime
Now write sentences that complete the following prompts:
My soul chose my parents in order:
a) to help me learn the following lessons:
b) to give me the following opportunities:

My soul chose my time of incarnation in order:
a) to help me learn the following lessons:
b) to give me the following opportunities:

My soul chose my gender in order:
a) to help me learn the following lessons:
b) to give me the following opportunities:

My soul chose my body type including the colour of my skin in order:
a) to help me learn the following lessons:
b) to give me the following opportunities:

My soul chose the following themes that challenge me both positively and negatively:

My soul helped to bring about the following important and significant synchronistic meetings and happenings in my life:

My soul gave me the following gifts and aptitudes from which I have learned:

I believe my soul work to be concerned with the following themes:

The things in my life I would most like to change through either circumstantial or attitudinal change are:

It may take some time to respond to all these points, and you may need to enrich your perspectives further by reading some of the following chapters before you can fully do so. As you continue and add to these reflections you will have a growing sense of important items that are present in your soul contract. Becoming aware of these will help you to notice them more clearly as ingredients in your life pattern. This in turn will enable your reference points for your own life planning and decision-making to be more creative and constructive as well as more consciously in tune with the purposes and intentions of your soul.

At different stages throughout this ongoing exploration, you might find it helpful to return to Exercise 1 (page 7) and to remind yourself of your personal image for the flame of your spirit burning safely within the chalice of your soul.

The following chapter looks at how you can recognise your life's teachers and how relationships of all kinds are very fertile ground for the business of working with your soul.

5

Learning from Relationships and Life's Teachers

As well as the circumstances of your birth, your soul uses many different life situations to put you in touch with the dilemmas and challenges you need to resolve in order to bring about your conscious learning in each incarnation. One of the richest arenas for soul work and evolution is through relationships of all kinds. There are many teaching situations in life that arise from life happenings and incidents, but life's teachers are also the *people* you meet and with whom you interact, those you love, find difficult or challenging, perhaps seriously dislike, or who even cause you to feel, and to have to deal with, the difficult and negative emotion of hatred.

Recognising life's teachers

You will usually have made a soul or higher self agreement, prior to incarnation, with your major life teachers. Such agreements are usually about interactions that will further your soul's search for knowledge, experience and balance. Your birth family, whether you eventually decide they are true soul companions or mainly chosen for genetic reasons (see Chapter 4), are almost certain to be teachers in your life. It follows with all of your life's teachers that the teaching that takes place may not be a one-way flow, but an exchange. The well-known saying 'to teach is to learn' is very appropriate here.

Karmic teachers

Your karmic, or soul, teachers are those who move you emotionally and touch you deeply. They may alter the course of your life either positively or negatively, but unmistakably. Their presence in your life may cause you to change direction, be jolted out of complacency, turn love into hate or vice versa. They may stir up whirlpools in previously calm waters and you may do the same for them. Where it is essential to your soul's intentions, and therefore to your soul contract, that things need to be very clearly learned, then you may meet more than one intense teacher so that certain issues or life themes will be presented and re-presented to you until you are very aware of them and no longer get caught up in them as obstacles on your path.

You can be sure, then, that when you continue to meet similar issues or dilemmas in life, your soul is endeavouring to awaken you to important work on hand. But equally it may be endeavouring to help you to step over that threshold between retributive and redemptive soul work as explained in Chapter 3.

Sally's story

The main teachers for Sally were very much of the challenging variety. They were the men in her life. She was an only child of parents who had divorced when she was six years old, and although she had maintained some childhood contact with her father, he had seemed to want to see less and less of her as she grew through adolescence into adulthood. He had given only minimal financial support to her mother to help in providing for her, and birthday and Christmas presents had either been forgotten or were less than generous.

Sally said that she counted her mum as one of, if not the best, of her close friends. Describing her mother as a best friend was a very telling statement. Sally felt very much that they were women in the world together. Until Sally was 14 her mother had maintained a stable home and tried to give her a home-based 'normal' childhood, but after that she had indicated that she needed to make a life of her own. She was not interested in a further partnership but in building an artistic career.

This had resulted in several house moves, and although there was always a place for Sally in her mother's home, it was not quite the same as having an enduring and solid home base and a father figure around. Her mother was definitely not 'mumsy'. On one level, Sally was proud of having a mother like this and was aware that even if her mother had moved into another partnership, any stepfather relationship would not be easy. There was no supportive male around and Sally's mother seemed to dismiss the need for one. Quietly, Sally dreamed of a secure household built around a secure and loving relationship – and this is what she was driven to seek for herself.

Sally's mother was a strong woman and Sally had a similar strength and capability in the world. Over and over again, she fell into relationships with weak men, who were attracted to Sally because they needed looking after. It seemed that she never saw it coming. Time and again she tried to make a life with a man who was too weak to give her the support she so very much wanted, so that she could relinquish the feeling of always having to do it herself and be the strong one. She longed for a man she could really lean on.

When Sally became interested in spiritual matters she looked at this pattern of re-presentation in her life and came to a realisation that her soul task must be about learning to be independent and to find her own inner wholeness and strength. As she saw this, she also saw how much she had already accomplished in terms of being her own person. Like her mother, she saw that life without a partner can also have its compensations.

Loosing the intense need for a supportive male and seeing that without commitments she actually had a desirable freedom and getting to the point where she no longer *needed* a man in her life seemed to free things up. Soon after this realisation she met just the man she had always hoped for. She saw the weak, betraying males as her life's teachers. She was prepared to go on alone, but because she had learned and seen the lesson in her life's presentations and re-presentations, the 'sacrifice' was no longer required of her. When she met the man of her dreams, she realised that if she had met him earlier, she would have related to him in a very different way that probably would also not have worked out for either of them.

Doors opening and closing: the power of synchronicity

Life's teachers open or close doors for you. A partner or dearly loved one can bring you confidence and joy in life. A seemingly chance encounter may lead to a long-term loving relationship. Wherever you go, at every moment, you may meet someone who will show you a new avenue of opportunity.

Equally, an unexpected meeting may turn out to be one that stops you in your tracks or brings you heartache and difficulty. Such people and encounters will have been put in your way, as surely as you will have been put in their way through the planning of your souls, in order to bring each of you some kind of awareness and awakening. Such meetings manifest through the power of synchronicity, which is linked to your soul's wider plan of action.

When groups come together for workshops or courses, the subtle as well as the more obvious significances and synchronicities that occur for those particular people, seemingly gathered together by chance at that particular time, have often been noticed and pondered with a sense of awe and wonder. Lasting friendships may be formed, a sense of spiritual or soul recognition may be celebrated, life partners may meet, working alliances made, challenges recog-nised and lessons learned all on the basis of being drawn to the same place at the same time to study something of mutual interest. The sense of something meaningful happening that is coming from that higher and mysterious level of planning, at which our souls excel, can become virtually palpable.

Some of your soul or life teachers may be actual career teachers that you have met during your years of formal education. For most people there is at least one teacher or formal educator who can be described as being brilliant at their job. Usually, such gifted individuals can inspire young minds, give confidence and understanding and demonstrate the true joys of learning. To be taught by them is to sense that they have a special interest in you as an individual. They make you feel cared for and that running an extra mile or so with you is their pleasure. In return you will probably, almost without thinking about it, make extra effort for them, in order not to 'let them down', or you may discover a shared joy in the process of teaching and learning.

The teachers you meet beyond the regular world of education may be recognised as having similar qualities. Learning with, and from, such people is gentle, supported, inspired and fun. It is the sort of experiential learning that enables you and others to celebrate life's journey together.

Continuing to identify life's teachers

It might be that not all the teachers from your formal education or elsewhere in life have taught you through dedication and inspiration. Let your reflections dwell on the way you were taught and the way in which you learned. Have you responded best to those who gently lead, inspire and harmoniously facilitate your learning? Or do you rather tend to respond to, and secretly respect more, those who give you a hard time and challenge you?

Recognising the various ways in which you learn and what it takes to make you note or react can be one way of improving your ability to work with your soul. If you tend to respond to teachers who are harsh taskmasters, then, when your soul wants you to learn, it may have little choice but to cause you to meet with life tutors of this kind or to use the 'kicks from behind' and 'knocks on the head' methods for getting your attention. If you work at becoming more sensitive and biddable in your learning, or come to recognise, as Sally did (page 55), that there is a lesson to learn, then such discordant re-presentations can cease. Conflict is not the preferred teaching method of your soul, but sometimes it can be the only way in which to awaken you to the need for change and reflection.

Your soul's duty to you and all the other beads on its thread is to see that work is done. If you tend to learn or change only through life's symbolic knocks on the head or kicks from behind then *you* may have to change before the way in which you receive life's lessons can be changed.

The perfect partner

Naturally, one of the most common areas asked about by people who come for guidance from Gildas is that of close relationships. It is natural to long to meet your perfect partner or your twin soul – the person we all long for, who we can be in total harmony with and who will know that the deepest secrets of our being can be shared. The most frequent relationship questions asked are about twin souls or soul mates and whether, how, and when they might be met. As explained in Chapter 2, the soul thread has two strands, like a double-stranded necklace joined at the clasp. Twin souls are personality beads from the parallel thread. Soul mates are personality beads, incarnate at the same time as you, from the same thread as yourself.

The generally understood interpretation of a twin soul relationship is that it is one where there need be no reservation. When you are in relationship together you totally remove from each other's lives any sense of that basic loneliness of the human condition that so many people feel. Twin souls do indeed exist. Some people do indeed meet up with them and live happily ever after, but, contrary to common expectation, such a fairytale ending is the exception rather than the rule, especially in our present times.

It may be disconcerting and disappointing to realise that you are unlikely to meet your twin soul, or other half, in your present incarnation. Yet once you know and understand this, your discontent and longing may be put to rest, as your expectations of the people you need to meet in life as part of your soul's contract for work to be done will become more realistic or informed. Partners in life, who are other than your twin soul, offer the perfect opportunity for the soul to put you alongside your most gifted or most exacting teachers and learning situations.

Alternative sexuality and the soul

As explained in Chapter 2, the thread of the soul that is yin (or feminine principle) and the thread of the soul that is yang (or masculine principle) each put out personality beads of both sexes into incarnation, and so it is possible to come to a wider spiritual understanding of alternative sexuality. Our society has tended to regard heterosexuality as the norm. That is not necessarily the standpoint of the soul. People of my generation (I was born in 1938) have seen great changes in legislation and society in general regarding homosexuality. Recently it became possible for couples of the same sex to enter into a legally binding and recognised union in a formal ceremony. In this, it would seem that society has become more compassionate, less judgemental and *perhaps* more spiritual or soul-conscious in its approach to relationships.

The full, more complex illustration of the soul necklace gives us the vision of a yin strand and a yang strand, each putting out personality beads into incarnation. Beads from each can be of either gender. It follows, then, that soul mates (beads incarnate from the same thread) and twin souls, (one bead from each thread), can easily be of the same gender and in incarnation at the same time. If they meet, they will have a powerful urge, whatever their gender, to be in relationship with each other.

From this view of the soul it can also be seen that a bead from the yin thread of the soul, in incarnation as a male, might strongly feel, and relate to, its feminine principle core and vice versa. This does not always happen when an incarnate personality bead takes on a gender that is opposite to its core principle, but it may. These considerations give a spiritual basis to add to or to consider alongside any psychological explanation of many gender issues and variations. Such choices have a special agenda within the learning curve of the soul.

Higher meaning in difficult relationships

Your family of origin is chosen by your soul to provide the major setting, support and/or spur for your life's soul work. Your parents, siblings and relatives may be nurturers, teachers, providers of opportunity, healers and/or challengers. Your soul may have arranged for you to be born surrounded by the people and circumstances that will set you gently on your journey – or it may have opted for, or been forced to resort to, more stringent methods or conditions.

Whether members of your genetic family of origin or not, those individuals who, on earth, seem to be your harshest taskmasters, may also be very close to you at a soul level. In the interests of learning your important lessons sooner rather than later, you may, before incarnation, have called on those who, from a soul level of connectedness and loving closeness understand the soul work that you are incarnating to do, to meet you in incarnation and to be your mentors or challengers. The confrontational roles they play for you on the stage of life may often evolve from that mysterious level of love that can agree to hurt or confront you, a loved one, in the interests of your soul purpose. There can even be a mutual evolutionary process and an intertwined soul purpose between you both.

It can be painful to be the catalyst, or to stand alongside and watch another's deep learning experiences or confrontations. Nevertheless, sometimes, at the highest level, it is *only* those you love and who love you the most who are able to make such sacrifices for you – or you for them. It is not always correct to assume that those with whom we clash in life, or those we betray or are betrayed by, are at the soul level in opposition to us. They may be soul family, soul mates or even your twin soul cooperating with your soul agenda to accelerate the learning or soul work required (see Brian's story on page 66).

Human relationships and soul work

The whole spectrum of human relationships is a powerful arena for working out learning processes of all kinds. We all long for closeness, love and understanding. Loneliness and isolation are foreign to human nature and are recognised as two of the greatest trials a human can endure. In relating to others, you discover the best and worst about yourself. Any inability or seeming failure in the field of human relationships is a potent trigger for self-searching. Relationship difficulties are one of the most common reasons that bring people into counselling.

If you are without friends and significant others you will be motivated to seek change. The grain of sand in the oyster shell becomes the precious pearl, and your soul knows this well. Irritation, unease, even dis-ease cause you to seek ways of moving on. Choices and decisions on life's path fuel your awareness. Presenting you with the challenge that motivates change is one of the means by which your soul intervenes or pre-plans for its work with you and yours with it. Your fellow humans, who cause you to react and interact, are your greatest teachers or catalysts. It is easy to model yourself on those who inspire you and whom you love and are loved by, but those who oppose, criticise, reject or betray you are also movers and shakers. When licking your wounds turns to recognition of this you will begin to understand more about the intricacies of your soul's plans and intentions.

Transformation in relationships

Much soul work is achieved where there is a transformation in relationships. Couples working through marriage or partnership difficulties *do* come back from points of despair and imminent separation to find that the best is yet to come. Families *can* get through periods of family rows and near rifts to realise a greater closeness. Creative compromises in relationships *do* happen. The path may be difficult and painful for a while, but resolution, and more, can be achieved. This is soul work in action. Yet soul work also happens when things cannot be worked out or resolved. Hard-won success can be very satisfying, but accepting that things cannot be changed may also open doors to new experience for all concerned.

The times when everything ticks along nicely tend to fade into relative insignificance whereas the troughs and peaks come most easily to memory. Things you can do or accomplish easily may be taken for granted. Obstacles, challenges, frustrations and difficulties are demanding of the life skills you already have or are the means whereby you develop other life skills and emotional and spiritual maturity. Reflecting on difficult predicaments you have been in or confrontations you have had with people in your life, and understanding the lessons you have learned from them, can often be difficult and painful. You may even realise that you carry or have carried the results of difficult encounters in your body, as symptoms or illness. (Illness as soul work is more fully considered in Chapter 8.)

Handling crises

The Chinese glyph for 'crisis' consists of two characters. One is the character for 'danger' and the other the character for 'opportunity'. When working with your soul it is desirable to develop the ability to see opportunities rather than dangers whenever crises present themselves. In this way you can come to know yourself not as a victim of your soul's planning but as a co-creator with it, and an ambassador for it. Recognising as teachers those who have brought you difficult relationship experiences, as well as naming the lessons they have taught or are teaching you, can help you avoid identifying yourself with being a powerless victim of circumstance.

Unfinished business

Resolution or transformation may not be possible in every difficult relationship situation. The wounds of betrayal, abandonment or rejection can be deep and disabling. You may be willing to work at something, but the other person or people involved may not. Soul work is certainly not selfish, although it *is* about enabling yourself to live as fully as possible. It is sometimes not only permissible but also right to walk away from a crippling relationship problem. Even if you feel that what you have been experiencing is a work of learning assigned to you by your soul, it may not always be possible to work right through it in the sense of 'getting it right' or bringing it into harmony. If someone with whom you are endeavouring to work on unfinished business is not able to respond to, or meet you in your efforts at resolution; or if there is some situation in your life where you feel you are repeatedly 'beating your head against a brick wall', then letting the situation eat away at your life may mean that you create a weight to carry or an obstacle on your own path. When the struggle really wears you down it may be time to give yourself permission to move on.

You can deal with unfinished business simply by declaring that it has reached stalemate and that you intend to move on from it. To walk away from an impasse can bring the opportunity to refocus more creatively. Your decision or choice in such a situation might enable or release others to be able to do the same.

The tasks your soul presents can be resolved or transformed indirectly as well as directly. Walking away from a gridlock situation can bring about release for all concerned. Analysis, understanding, owning your hurt and your ability to hurt others, as well as finding a solution that frees up energy, all help to make sure that you do not live your life either re-wounding yourself or others or in continual pain from wounds that are too raw to heal. These are choices that are for you to make at the personality level as part of working cooperatively with your soul.

Wounding from relationships

In my practice I see a lot of people who are dealing with wounding caused by relationships. The first focus is always on the psychological understanding, healing and decision-making that belong to the here and now. Part of the healing may eventually come from insight into why your soul might have put such encounters on your life's way. The work of self-healing, understanding and moving on, has a deeper and more satisfying significance when things are put into a wider perspective. Broader understanding helps you to tap into, or discover your deepest reserves of, emotional and spiritual strength.

The dimension of what has gone before

There may never be complete and full understanding of what has gone before, with all the i's dotted and the t's crossed, but learning to sense the aims of your soul from the pattern of your life can gradually bring you more of those 'Ahaaa!' moments of insight that Michael had during his session with Gildas (page 25). Especially with the help of the exercises in this book you can learn to enhance your ability to think as your soul thinks and to appreciate the way it makes its plans.

As you realise that present difficulties have wider causes, it becomes easier to think in the context of the longer period of total evolution as different from the normally expected present lifespan. This can take some pressure off, as you come to accept that you are not a lone worker for your soul and that not every task you may perceive yourself as having been given has to be started from scratch, and begun and finished within your present 'three-score years and ten'.

You are like a participant in a relay event, where a previous personality bead hands you the torch of the spirit so that you can travel the next leg of the journey. Equally, having done your part, you will eventually hand the torch on. Keeping it burning and keeping moving are the more likely items of your brief, rather than to be seeking completion or perfection.

Finding greater depth in life's challenges

In these pages I am encouraging you not to see cause and effect as a mechanism that brings about certain punishment for past misdemeanours, but it is also true that much of the soul's programming is actually based on what has gone before and what therefore needs to come after, in order to balance or compensate. To be rejected or betrayed will always hurt. Knowing that you are working on such things as items in your soul contract can bring greater depth into how you regard the meaning of your life's challenges. It is possible to gain a transpersonal and symbolic perspective that nurtures and motivates survival and helps minimise scar tissue. Dealing with soul-contract issues can make present life situations seem more intense, but *accepting* that something is bigger than the immediate and obvious restores a sense of context and proportion.

The exercises at the end of each chapter are aimed at helping you towards a progressive revelation of items in your soul contract. In the next chapter there is more about *methods* of achieving the life changes you may wish to make. Before that, Brian's story will illustrate and expand on some of the information given in this chapter, and Exercise 5 will help you to acknowledge and celebrate your life's teachers.

I met Brian when he signed up for a workshop dealing with exploring and mapping the territory of our inner worlds and landscapes. Such mapping can help in developing a closer contact with your soul as well as with those other dimensions where you may meet with your guides, guardian angel and other subtle and invisible helpers.

Brian's story

Brian wanted more contact with his soul, or a deeper understanding of the way in which the soul communicates its purposes because he was in great distress about a relationship that it seemed could not, and would not, work out for either of them. He and a very much older woman had fallen deeply in love with each other. Lillian had older children who were both married with young families, making Lillian a grandmother with four grandchildren. Her son was two years older and her daughter just one year younger than Brian.

Brian was 28 years old. On leaving school he had gone to work in an accountancy office, but was currently re-training as a social worker. He and Lillian had met at a residential yoga weekend. They had been irresistibly drawn to each other but now found themselves facing a seemingly insoluble dilemma.

Lillian's husband had died in a tragic road accident some six years previously. Lately her children had been encouraging her to look for another relationship to help her move on from her grief and to enrich and broaden her life once more. She had undertaken a broader spectrum of activities such as the yoga weekend with this in mind. Having met Brian and fallen in love with him almost instantaneously she now did not feel comfortable with introducing him to her family as a very close friend, and certainly not as her new man. Their time together, as far as she was concerned, had to be of the nature of secret assignations but she also felt that she could not carry on much longer with this sort of deception. Lillian was highly involved with her family, and keeping secrets from them as well as the sense of shame she was beginning to feel, which was so diametrically opposed to her love and joy, had made her determined to end the relationship.

Brian insisted that all these difficulties could be overcome. He had no real family ties. He did not need to justify his life decisions to anyone else. His family had never been close. He had an older sister who had married an Australian and gone to live in her husband's home country. Brian's retired parents lived in a quiet market town in the south of England and had a life full of local activities and interests. His mother and father had always looked forward to early retirement and had worked hard to achieve it. They were very close as a couple and although they had been good parents they were less involved in the lives and decisions of their adult offspring.

Brian was so much in love with Lillian that he felt he could face every obstacle that might be put in their way. He wanted to shout his love and delight from the rooftops. He felt that a relationship that moved them both so much and seemed so right when they were able to be together must, despite the age difference, have been made in heaven. He was completely certain that Lillian was his twin soul and that therefore, surely, they were meant to be together. He felt that if they could take the plunge and be together openly, although others might view their relationship negatively, like a 'nine-day wonder', it would not take long for all difficulties to melt away.

Lillian fully acknowledged the spiritual quality in her relationship with Brian. Her marriage had been a good one and she had loved her husband deeply, but now she felt something extra. She described it as a sense of 'coming home', of feeling totally in harmony with someone beyond anything she had ever experienced or even expected before. Although Lillian had never previously given serious thought to such things as reincarnation and the soul, she did have a deep feeling that this meeting with Brian could certainly be the renewal of an old relationship. She agreed that, in some sense, they must have met before or always known each other. She felt that they were of one and the same substance.

Lillian's realisation that the realistic and practical difficulties standing in the way of having a thoroughly open and acknowledged relationship with Brian were overwhelming and too difficult to overcome was a painful one. While acknowledging the extreme grief and frustration that both would feel, she felt that the only way forward was to go their separate ways. She knew that for her to be openly in relationship with Brian would cause enormous family upset. She was unwilling to be a catalyst for this at a time when she felt they had only just entered more tranquil waters after all the family upset that had resulted from her husband's tragic death.

Brian and Lillian's love was deep, but they had now reached an impasse and were deeply angry with each other. Lillian spoke of the sacrifice she knew she must make and the one she was unable to make. Brian complained that he *was* the actual sacrifice. Lillian felt that Brian was far from truly empathising with her dilemma. Brian said that if she really loved him there would not be a dilemma. He proclaimed that if their souls had allowed them to meet in this present lifetime it must be that they were *meant* to be together. He felt that he could never feel whole again without Lillian beside him. Lillian said that perhaps their souls had deeper and maybe harder lessons intended for them in allowing them to meet and recognise each other. Brian said that if this was so, he was very angry with his soul for putting him through such frustration.

Learning more about the complexity of the soul and its purposes from the workshops that he attended enabled Brian to begin to modify his anger towards his soul, and also towards Lillian, but he still hoped to find a way through that would see him and Lillian living happily ever after. Eventually they decided to come together to consult with my guide, Gildas, and to ask for his perspective on the challenges and dilemmas they were facing.

Their main needs were to know from Gildas why, if it was going to be so difficult to be together, they had actually met in this current lifetime. They wanted to know how far they could justify disruption to the lives of others by giving priority to their own need to be together. They also wanted to know whether Gildas could set their present dilemma in any kind of context with their previous lives, and so help them to see some of the deeper lessons to be learned from their situation.

Gildas very rarely takes on the role of telling people what to do. He gives another perspective and helps in seeing options and the possible consequences attendant on those options. He endeavours to point out the choices the soul may be offering in any given situation. There is often more than one possible soul agenda, and the choice and responsibility for the consequences, either positive or negative, are up to the incarnate personality. It is in this way that you have the freedom to make your own life decisions and give a chosen shape to your living, rather than seeking to be totally lived by your soul.

On this occasion Gildas told Brian and Lillian that when twin souls are in incarnation together in the same or similar geographic area, they have almost a magnetic attraction for each other. Thus their meeting may not have been by synchronous arrangement of their joint soul, but rather as a result of this energetic magnetism. On the other hand, he also felt that their soul may have been offering them some testing options. He saw these as being related to a similar dilemma that they had faced in a previous lifetime, where they had met without the difficulty of the age difference they were now facing but nevertheless already having other commitments. In that lifetime, they had chosen to be together and sever the other obligations with all the upset and consequences involved.

As always, Gildas said that sometimes it is justifiable to make choices that lead to your being a catalyst for change of attitude in others and even for challenge and confrontation. He empathised with Lillian who was the more forcibly faced with such a dilemma. He pointed out that the difference in their ages, although making no difference to their love and soul recognition, could be a factor designed by their soul to make them consider a different choice in this present lifetime from the one they had made in the previous one he had seen.

He agreed that whatever decision they came to, a degree of sacrifice would be involved. He pointed out that in the growth and strengthening of the soul, sacrifice is a theme that has to be learned about and dealt with.

Gildas was not able to offer a cut-and-dried solution to their dilemmas, but they both said that he had sharpened the perspective for them and that what he had said would help them to make a more responsible and considered decision about how to proceed with their lives.

Brian felt particularly sobered by what Gildas had said, especially in view of the stated karmic background to their dilemma. He began to empathise more deeply with Lillian's feelings about the effect their relationship would have on her family. Lillian felt that if she had abandoned commitments in one lifetime, she certainly did not want to do so again, and although her offspring had lives of their own, she still felt deep responsibilities to them and her grandchildren.

Brian finished his social work course and obtained a job in a far away town. They agreed that they both wanted to keep up their interest in yoga and would give themselves the luxury of two residential yoga courses each year as a way of keeping in touch. They knew that although agreeing to meet regularly was, in one sense, a gratification, it might also exacerbate the pains of their dilemma, but it was something they both wanted and felt they would help each other to deal with.

It was difficult for them both, but eventually Brian was able to say to me that he realised he was at a very different life stage from Lillian. At one time he had felt that despite that he could not live successfully without her. Now he felt glad that he had accepted her need to fulfil her own obligations and he was able to live more fully, simply knowing that the one who made him feel more whole and more aware of his soul *was* there in incarnation at the same time as he was. He felt that he would certainly never actively seek another relationship in his present lifetime, but was ready to accept that his soul/higher self might eventually decide to present him with such a dilemma. He would take life as it came and trust that he would be presented with the right opportunities as well as the right challenges for his journey of working with his soul.

Lillian treasured what she had been allowed to glimpse but felt easier in herself and her self-value because she had embraced sacrifice. She also had to acknowledge that there had been a truth in what Brian had said in his anger when he had spoken about being sacrificed. In some senses he *had* been a very poignant sacrifice in the process of the soul's work and learning, but both of them were now coming to recognise the joint sacrifice that had been necessary. They had reached something of a creative, however painful, compromise in their resolution of their dilemma.

Brian and Lillian both felt that they had experienced passion in every sense of the word. Despite the emotional pain, stress and sense of loss, however, they felt more in touch with their joint soul and more mutually participant in making a choice of how best to work with, and for, its evolution.

Exercises on recognising your life teachers

The first exercise in this section helps to continue and reinforce the work you will have already done by following Exercises 1–4. The emphasis here is on seeing the people who have made a notable impression on your life and who have thus become your life teachers. You are also asked to reflect on the times when you feel you may have been a teacher for others. Exercise 6 is a ceremony to celebrate and affirm your insights about your life teachers and your part as a teacher. Before you begin, read through Preparing for the Exercises on page 5.

Exercise 5: *more clearly identifying life's teachers*

Once again you will need your special notebook or some paper and coloured pencils or pastels.

This is an informal reflective exercise that is not intended to be completed within a particular time. If you think about this regularly, even in the back of your mind, over a period of days or weeks, it will help you to see certain interactions with people in your life in a different way. It will also help you to identify more of the ways in which your soul reveals its work agenda for, or contract with, you in this present lifetime.

Remember that not every insight will come from the more formal sessions or approach. As you get further into this work, and follow the exercises given at the end of each chapter, related ideas and insights will tend to 'pop up' as you go about the routine tasks of your life. It makes sense then, to try to have your notebook with pen attached and crayons conveniently near to you as often as possible while you are going through the process of learning to understand your soul contract and how to work more clearly with your soul.

Each time you take the formal approach to this exercise, read through the reflections and life reviews you have accumulated as a result of the previous exercises.

1. Make sure that you will be comfortable and undisturbed. Find your comfortable position.

2. Focus on the rhythm of your breathing. Be aware of each in-breath and out-breath, not trying to alter its tempo in any specific way, but allowing it to find its natural level and flow.

3. Sense your breath as coming in and out at the 'petals' of your heart centre or chakra (life energy centre). This lies in the centre of your body and aura on the same level as your physical heart (see Glossary).

4. As your regular breathing helps your heart chakra to open, get a sense of entering your own inner space or dimension.

5. In this relaxed state, and having read the material you have noted from previous exercises, centre on the people in your life who, in this moment, come most powerfully to mind. Do not *try* to remember anyone or anything in particular, just keep breathing the heart breath as memories or impressions of people flow into your awareness. At this stage try not to judge or censor what comes, but simply allow your psyche to reveal what it chooses.

6. In this heart-centred state take your notebook or the paper you have at hand and note down memories of the people who are coming to mind. Write their names, what you felt, or still feel about them, whether positive or negative, whether you are still in contact with them, how you lost contact or anything else concerning them that seems noteworthy at this time.

7. Write key words as well as more wordy descriptions. You might want to write words in different colours or use colour to draw patterns as you recall and record feelings and emotions.

8. Write down, too, where you were in your life when you met these people and any life changes you made because of meeting them or that they may have made because of meeting you.

9. Note whether or not you recognised these people as important at the time you met them or whether you are now seeing their importance with hindsight.

10. Don't forget to include those people who have challenged you negatively as well as the ones who helped to move your life forwards or into a different direction.

11. Reflect also on people in your life who you feel may have had awakenings, new experiences or challenges as a result of meeting you. Are you aware of being a catalyst for change in another person's life, either through special contact, friendship, love or through a challenge *you* may have presented to them? Again write key words, or use colours to express something about these meeting points and experiences.

12. When you have spent between 20 and 30 minutes in this heart-centred, heart-breathing state, close your notebook or put your paper aside. Now feel your feet firmly on the ground, become aware of your everyday surroundings and walk around a little; make yourself a drink, step outside and breathe fresh air, or do something else that is practical and grounding, bringing you firmly back into your present everyday world.

13. Now, or later, you may want to open your notebook again, or look at your papers and contemplate the impressions and memories that came to you in your heart-centred reflections. Now, in more cognitive mode make two lists:
    a. Teachers in my life and things I have learned from them.
    b. Situations where I have been a catalyst for others and things they may have learned from me.

14. Finally, keep reflecting on the effects people or relationships of all kinds have had on your life. Consider the perspective that where relationships and encounters are memorable for whatever reason, they have, most probably, been orchestrated by your soul as part of your soul contract for this present lifetime.

15. Reflect on how well you feel you have assimilated or identified the lessons given out by your personal life teachers. Be particularly aware of any re-presentations in your life of similar situations.

Exercise 6: *celebration and affirmation*

This is a ceremony rather than an exercise and you will need to sense when you are ready to perform it. It is particularly suitable to use alongside Exercise 5, in order to celebrate and affirm any insights you have had about your life teachers and your part as a teacher in the lives of others. It can also be used or adapted for affirming other recognitions regarding your soul contract and your progression with it.

1. Look through all your notes and insights to date and decide if there are realisations you now need to take action on in your life, and then specify one or two, with clear wording. These would include things you need to let go of, things you need to celebrate and energise, things you are now working to achieve a clearer perspective about or things that feel 'stuck' and need creative or inspired solutions.

2. Prepare an altar-like space either indoors or outdoors. Indoors you might clear a small table or space on a shelf. Put a cloth on it if possible. It is good for such ceremonials

to have all four elements represented. You could arrange some crystals or ordinary stones on the cloth and/or have a small plant in a pot to represent earth. A candle or night-light in a suitable container gives you fire, a feather can represent air, and you can include some water in a small bowl or other container.

3. When all is ready and you know the issues you are working with, surround yourself with the heart breath by focusing on the rhythm of your breathing and becoming aware of each in-breath and out-breath; without trying to alter your breathing tempo in any specific way, allow it to find a natural flow.

4. Sense your breath as coming in and out at the 'petals' of your heart centre or chakra so opening and activating your heart energy.

5. Light your candle, and watch its flame for a while. As the flame burns upwards, invoke a connection with your soul. Look at the issues you have written down and ask for the help you need, either to let go, move on, find solutions or to celebrate realisations.

6. Thank your soul for its contract with you in this present lifetime and re-affirm any intentions you have to cooperate more fully with it by making it more conscious.

7. Sit in contemplation for not more than 20 minutes and then feel the ground beneath your feet. Put a cloak of light with a hood right around you, blow out your candle and return to your normal everyday activities.

8. Blowing out the candle is part of the ceremony, and not just a safety measure. It affirms that you have thought about these things and the actions that you want to take and that a new phase is now beginning.

Chapter 6 looks more closely at the things that you can do, and self-help tools you can use in order to build insights about your soul contract, to make growing closer to your soul more realistic and to implement creative change in your life.

6

Tools for Deeper Understanding

In this chapter I want to look at some of the practicalities of working more consciously with your soul's purposes. I want to answer the questions, 'Which knowledge and practices can help me to instigate those changes in my life that will help me to feel in co-creatorship with my soul?' and 'How can I help myself to turn my life around so that it is not one in which things just happen to me in a seemingly random and unconnected sequence of events?'

In life, three of our main responses to happenings are to *react*, to *interact* and to *act*. There is an important difference between reaction and interaction and their relationship to action. In working effectively with your soul it is important to ponder upon this.

Reaction can send you off at a tangent or polarity and is generally not thought out or considered.

Interaction is a dialogue and can enable you to have a more creative input into your life choices as well as a more conscious vertical connection to the vibrancy of your soul. In some senses *reaction* can lead to *actions* that come from an impulsive response made on the rebound.

Action is what you *do* about any given situation and will be more wisely based when it is informed by interaction and consideration rather than by impulse. Learning to bypass or sideline *reaction* in favour of *interaction* can lead to calmer ways of understanding why certain things happen to you as and when they do and result in wise action when dealing with life's surprises.

There are a number of tools or areas of knowledge that can support your work with your soul and help you to develop a deeper understanding of, and interaction with, your soul's purposes. The following pages name, explain and discuss these tools as an aid to helping you to know and choose which might be the most important for you to use at any of your crossroads in life.

As you work with this book, you are undertaking psychological and spiritual growth, which you may eventually want to use as a more formal way of underpinning and supporting changes you feel drawn to make.

Tool 1: psychological and spiritual growth

Although they are grouped here under one heading, there are both differences and meeting points between psychological and spiritual growth

Psychology is the study of human nature. Study or therapy that leads to greater understanding of self can be of great importance in working with your soul. In Chapter 4 the question of 'nature or nurture?' has already been raised. Psychological understanding of self can help in differentiating between these two important aspects of your development and therefore of different aspects of your soul contract.

Spiritual growth is less mainstream. It also differs from religious practice, although may, for some, include it. Spiritual growth includes the search for higher meaning and purpose in life, which, when applied directly to self, can nurture your growth process and inform its aims. Working with your soul is a form of spiritual journeying and includes the need to come to know and observe yourself in minute but special ways.

Included in the field of spiritual growth is an area that I usually refer to as 'esoteric spirituality'. It is that sphere of spiritual growth and study that has firm beliefs in 'life beyond life', interaction with discarnate communicators, reincarnation, the vivid reality and interpenetration of other planes of consciousness and the ability to access and interact with them. I describe it as 'esoteric' because it has its own vocabulary and contributory or derivative areas of study that include other realms or spheres, karma, chakras, subtle bodies, healing, dowsing, astrology, channelling and mediumship (see Glossary).

Counselling and therapy

Psychological counselling or psychotherapy is useful if you reach a crisis in your life or feel that you need support in your journey to self-knowledge and in learning exactly what makes you 'tick'. It can give specific help and support if you are depressed or anxious about some-thing or are looking to change your habitual behavioural responses in order to avoid repetitive presentation of similar life dilemmas. This latter work is intrinsically related to working with your soul.

In counselling or therapy you will usually look at the circum-stances of your present life and the things that have happened to you. Traditionally, the things to be explored will include details about your family and early life, your relationship to your parents and siblings, the ways in which you manage your life and bearing, and the changes you are hoping to make. The work of therapy seeks, by understanding the obstacles that you have encountered in life, to enable you to take self-responsibility and to live without undue hang-ups and limitations. It aims to help you to know and accept yourself and to give your being full permission to blossom. By enabling you to have a better understanding of yourself, therapy can help you towards attitudinal change and may support you during phases in which you implement circumstantial change.

The role of transpersonal therapy

Transpersonal psychology addresses the spiritual needs and aspirations of human beings as well as the behavioural patterns and considerations. My own therapeutic training is as a transpersonal psychotherapist. In transpersonal therapy, focus is given to the importance of symbols, finding meaning in life, and to being creatively fulfilled in living, relating and making choices. It is of especial help in learning to work with your soul, as it encourages the search for higher meaning and holds symbolic thinking about the dilemmas of life as being of prime importance. It also includes, as many psychologies or therapies do not, the concept and reality of spirit and soul as important life dimensions and perspectives. One of the great originators – and even after his death a continuing inspirer of transpersonal psychology – was C.G. Jung. He placed great emphasis on archetypes and archetypal patterns in personal and collective life. The place of archetypes in soul work and soul service is such an important, although quite complex, tool in working with your soul that it has the next chapter to itself.

Tool 2: thinking symbolically

Transpersonal psychology, or the transpersonal approach, can also help you to develop the important ability to think symbolically and honour symbols in your life. In getting to know how your soul communicates its purposes it is important to be able to 'think outside the box'.

The exercises given so far are there to help you to become more alert to inference, to be ready to follow intuitions and hunches, to ponder relationships, question all exchanges and take personal responsibility. At all times, but especially when life seems to be full of obstacles, challenges and setbacks, being able to interpret things symbolically can lead to a fuller sense of where you are in the total pattern of all that is.

The psychiatrist, Viktor Frankl, who experienced and wrote about the terrible privations of concentration camps, observed that even in the midst of such hardship and suffering some people were still able to find symbolic meaning. It was these individuals or groups who maintained a greater quality of mental, emotional, physical and spiritual health.

What are symbols?

The main definition of a symbol is that it is something that represents something else, and by so doing, brings a sense of wider and deeper meaning. Symbols are often pictorial or imaginative. C.G. Jung explains that symbols may be used as signs, but are also more than signs. For example, the familiar red cross on a white background is, in our society, a sign that 'first aid' is at hand. The *symbol* of the red cross holds a greater richness: on a white background it is both the sign of the crusaders and the flag of St George. A cross, red or otherwise, is an ancient pictorial illustration of the cardinal points. It can also illustrate the seasons of the year (spring, summer, autumn and winter) or our human make-up of mind, body, emotions and spirit. A sign has a single meaning; a symbol has multiple meanings.

Interpreting symbols

If you use your inner worlds, or study your dreams, all manner of images and symbols may appear. Try not to interpret your symbols by using the sort of symbol book that gives you an immediate or categorical definition such as 'a snake symbolises sex'. Remember that symbols will have a personal richness as well as more universal significance. C.G. Jung said, 'It is important to *have* a symbol', meaning that having the symbol is at least *as* important as being able to interpret it. When you learn to live alongside your symbols and to reflect on their meaning, they will gradually reveal more and more not only about themselves but also about why they have come to you at a particular time in your life and evolution.

The first level at which to explore a symbol is not by looking it up in a reference book but by making personal association to it. What does the symbol mean to *you*? Where and when have you seen it before? What do you associate directly with it? The symbol has come to *you*. It is *yours*. Looking into reference books is the next stage, which is known as amplification. There are several excellent symbol dictionaries (see Bibliography), which, instead of giving limited interpretations, look at each symbol from many angles and give you information about all the traditional meanings. Amplification can also mean asking friends if they have information on or suggestions to make about any of your symbols. If you explore your symbols with respect you will find the often-astonishing wealth and immeasurable depths of wisdom that each one can hold.

A personal story

In my early days of psychotherapy, I learned the importance of not going to the amplified meaning of a symbol before checking on the level of personal association. A client brought me a dream about a dragon that had laid two eggs. My mind immediately went to the way in which dragons are fierce, fiery and armoured and often need fighting and conquering. I felt that if this creature in her dream had laid two eggs, maybe there was a great deal in her psyche coming up to be confronted. Fortunately, just in time, I asked her for her personal associations to dragons.

She replied that the dragon brought back memories of a very arid phase of her childhood where her parents had lost everything and had been reduced to living, in the middle of winter, in a mobile home. 'Everything seemed cold, strange and hard,' she said, 'All my toys had accidentally gone into storage with the few other things that had been rescued. Then an aunt came to visit, and she brought a hand-knitted dragon that was colourful, soft and warm. It was a lifeline to me, and I still have it and hold it when life gets hard'. Her dream was not about challenges she had to face at all, but about softness and warmth in her life and the potential, in the dragon's eggs, for more of the same.

Thinking symbolically about life helps your dialogue with your soul to become clearer and may help you, even when you feel yourself to be 'in extremis' to find meaning in that which could otherwise overwhelm. There is more about this approach to soul work in Chapter 8, which looks at where, in this work, to place illness and the dark nights of the soul.

Tool 3: gathering the clues

Thinking symbolically can help to give you a clearer view of where your life fits into the chain of lives lived by previous incarnate beads from your soul stem. Remember that your life givens have multi-layered clues as to your soul contract for this present lifetime (see Chapter 4).

Tool 4: spiritual practice

You will find that some form of regular spiritual practice is helpful to becoming more 'soulful' or in touch with your soul work on a day-to-day basis. Your practice could be meditation, lighting a candle each morning and centring yourself for a few moments before the concerns of the day take over, or it could be breathing exercises, or choosing a thought for the day from an inspirational book or pack of cards (see Bibliography).

The practice of a daily life review is a deceptively simple but effective spiritual practice that can have far-reaching effects. At the end of each day ponder on the events of your day, either in your thoughts or by writing a list. First of all remember each event as an item on a simple list. After you have made this list go back over it to review your thoughts and emotions associated with each happening. You do not need to make a life review every day, but once or twice a week helps you to get a clearer sense of the way you are living your life in its present phase and to ponder on your reactions, interactions and actions.

It is important that you do not use the practice of daily life review to be over- judgemental or over-critical about yourself and your life in any negative sense. Gildas uses the phrase 'continuously assess yourself without either false pride or false modesty'. To achieve this you need to use another tool, which is that of cultivating the non-judgemental inner observer.

Tool 5: cultivate the non-judgemental inner observer

Within your being you will have belief systems and thought patterns that tend to rule your life and influence your choices. Some or most of these may be very positive, coming from the core of your being and based on your whole experience of making clear, creative and beneficial choices. Others may be rather more negative patterns based on 'shoulds' and 'oughts' ingested from parents and teachers or even from ideas of a judgemental God waiting to assess you at the end of your life.

The non-judgemental observer does not have a voice as such, but is a mirror offering you insight into how you have acted and what you have done. This insight is offered simply and without criticism. In the same way as when you look in a mirror to see how you are dressed and then make decisions about whether to alter some aspect of your attire or not, so the non-judgemental observer offers you the opportunity to see your life, reactions, interactions and actions clearly so that you can take the space in which to decide what you do and do not like. When you see clearly, you are then free to consider whether or not to arrange things differently, or perhaps to declare yourself well pleased with what you see. The non-judgemental inner observer is very different from the inner critic and merely offers you, in an informed way, the opportunity to reflect on what is happening and to change it if necessary.

Tool 6: attitudinal and circumstantial change

When you have a clear way of seeing yourself you will know when it is time to think about making attitudinal and circumstantial change.

Knowing how to make these changes can help you to feel more in control of your life and to move through the stages of retributive, redemptive and transcendent soul work (see Chapter 3).

Attitudinal and circumstantial change have also been mentioned in Chapter 3 and in Michael's story (page 25). Attitudinal change is when you seek to change your attitude or perspective on those things that you may see as an insurmountable obstacle or sense as a challenge that you don't feel equipped to meet and are unable to resolve. Circumstantial change is when you implement big life changes such as changing your job, going through a relationship break-up or moving to a new place to live. In terms of soul work, an urgent call on your resources to make either attitudinal or circumstantial change will often mark a very clear change from retributive soul work to redemptive soul work, as discussed in Chapter 3.

Facing confrontation or painful experience often promotes, inspires or brings energy for change. To some extent circumstantial and attitudinal change go hand in hand. Sometimes *only* attitudinal change may be possible, but it is also true to say that before circumstantial change can be made, a degree of attitudinal change must take place. Crisis can inspire, and your soul knows and uses this.

When you are in crisis and need to make either circumstantial or attitudinal change, it may be a time to seek help from someone who knows about spiritual growth and the messages of the soul (see Tool 1).

Thinking back to the Chinese glyph for crisis (see Handling Crises, page 63), the danger in crisis is that there can be a spiralling into depression, hopelessness and severe loss of meaning. The opportunity lies in the awakening of inner resources that may before have lain dormant and in using them to embrace and create positive change of either kind.

Two examples follow of people who have made mainly attitudinal or mainly circumstantial change in their lives.

Attitudinal change

At times when circumstances not only *seem* but actually *are* unalterable, flexible, creative and symbolic thinking can help. Things can be seen from a different perspective, put into a wider context and given the kind of meaning that clears frustration and brings a very different relationship to matters in hand. This is attitudinal change.

Miriam's story

A teacher and single parent, Miriam felt trapped in the educational system, but could see no way out at least for a number of years, because the teaching hours and a certain amount of flexibility suited her as a single parent. She felt tension building in her, as she realised that she did not want to be a teacher but a healer. She had begun to really dislike her identity as a teacher.

Miriam came for some short-term counselling and gradually began to see that there was a lot of opportunity for healing, in an implicit sense, alongside teaching and within the school environment. There was a duty of care for the children she taught and also in her relationship to the children's parents. By focusing more on this duty of care and on making her classroom a place of healing by the atmosphere she created there she could feel that the healer in her had some meaningful and positive outlet. She could also see her teaching career not just as a means to making single parenthood more acceptable by giving her more time to spend with her child.

As so often happens with attitudinal change, as Miriam came to realise that she did not have to deny the healer in her in favour of the teacher, a post of extra responsibility for pastoral care was created in the school where she worked. She applied for the post and was successful. Her caring abilities were officially recognised and she was given more opportunity to express them. The establishment was not exactly recognising her as a healer, but it was enough to support her own attitudinal change and calm her tension and frustration. She had not been able, at this time, to make a circumstantial change, but because her attitude had changed she no longer felt trapped. She knew that eventually her present responsibilities and limitations would change and now she could wait and plan patiently for the circumstantial change that she knew she would be able to implement at the right time.

In Miriam's story, of course, it is also possible to reflect on the role of the archetypes (see Chapter 7). The healer archetype was more important to Miriam than was the teacher. Circumstances just did not allow her to branch out into, or retrain for, healing work, but by focusing more on the healer anyway, Miriam felt more in harmony with the aspects of herself that she felt were most related to her life's purpose.

Circumstantial change

Martin's circumstantial change was forced upon him through the long terminal illness and the eventual death of his wife Joanne, which had happened about one year previously. When he came for counselling, he was still distraught with grief. He was being treated by his doctor for depression and had had some previous bereavement counselling.

Martin's story

Joanne and Martin had married in their early twenties and had been together for ten years. They were very close and had decided to spend time doing together the things they most enjoyed and to leave making a final decision about whether to have children or not until later. After six years of what Martin described as 'sheer delight', Joanne discovered a breast lump, which had tested positive for cancer. It was an aggressive type and, although in between bouts of treatment they had felt and hoped it might be in remission, there was always a setback such as the development of metastases.

Martin did everything he could to help Joanne through her illness, but eventually the cancer spread to her bones, her lungs and her brain. The oncologists finally said that there was nothing more they could do, even to give Joanne more time. As the deterioration started, Martin nursed Joanne devotedly until eventually she went into a hospice for respite care but died just one week later.

Now Martin was plagued by flashbacks to the terrible way Joanne had looked in her last days, by sadness and anger about her ravaged and mutilated body. After her funeral he had gone to stay with good friends in Spain, near the sea and the mountains, hoping that sun and sea and mountain air would help to heal him. They did not.

Martin was an engineer by profession and had quite a high-powered job. His firm had told him to take as much compassionate leave as he wished, but on his return from Spain he had felt the need to occupy himself and had returned to work and become something of a workaholic. He hated living in the lovely home he had shared with Joanne. He hated the daily routine without her, he dreaded leaving home in the mornings, although he did not want to stay there. He dreaded returning to the empty house in the evening. He didn't want to go out with friends and had not been feeding himself properly. He had made some plans to sell the house, but at the same time as wanting to get rid of it he couldn't bear to part with it. He hoped that eventually the house would enable him to dwell on the many happy times he and Joanne had had together, but he felt he was getting stuck in his grief rather than being able to relate to the healing that time is supposed to bring.

Martin was not religious but felt that he might possibly feel better if he could find some meaning to his and Joanne's suffering. He also said that if he *had* had a real belief in an afterlife he might well have been suicidal, because he would then have hoped to be immediately together with Joanne again.

I asked him what sort of things Joanne had said, when she knew that she was going to die. Martin reminisced about how she had thanked him for all the joy and love he had given her and the wonderful times they had enjoyed together. She told him that she hoped he would remember and honour those times, but also that he would be able to move on and find another love and sparkling quality of life again. He remembered that Joanne *had* had an unshakeable belief in the purpose and pattern of things and that although she was devastated to be leaving she had no regrets about her life. She foresaw that Martin would find it difficult to recover after she had gone, but said that she also believed that if she had to go, then it must mean that Martin had something to do or something to gain from the lack of ties he would have. Neither of them had brothers or sisters, and had each lost both parents at an early age. Indeed then, Martin had no ties and that was part of his problem in being unable to move through his depression and find new meaning in life.

As he talked, Martin gradually began to realise that if Joanne was right about an afterlife or continued existence, then she would be sad to see the state he was in now. In some ways it was still early days, but he felt unable to make plans or decisions at all. He also began to think that Joanne's belief in everything that happened in life having a purpose needed further thought. I lent him some of my books and some other books on belief in continued existence and the evolution of the soul.

Synchronicity played its part. Friends invited Martin for supper and for once he accepted. There he got talking to a young man who had done some voluntary service overseas during his gap year before going to university. Martin knew that developing countries could benefit from his own skills and he suddenly found the idea of 'service' very inspiring. Within a short time he had researched what he could do and where he could go. He put his house out to rent, rather than making the decision to sell it as yet, and went off to live in frugal conditions in developing countries to contribute his skills and give himself a new purpose in life.

Martin had been unable to make either attitudinal or circumstantial change. He had been trapped in deep grief. Once he had made even a little opening that let in a sense that life has more meaning than the daily round his thinking began to change. He realised that if Joanne was looking at him from some other plane, he might actually be burdening her with his own despair. This gave him the incentive to move on in a very courageous way and to use his unlooked-for 'freedom' to good purpose. I am not sure how far he would later put the events in his life into a full context of working with his soul, but feel that he might have been on the way to doing so.

Tool 7: subpersonalities – the many aspects within

Your psyche is rich and multi-dimensional. When asked how you feel about something or a decision you have to make, you may find yourself saying: 'Well part of me feels ... and another part feels ...' or, 'part of me wants to do ... and another part wants to ...'.

From the perspective of working with your soul, you can recognise that there are many personality beads on your soul thread, of which you are one. As an incarnate individual you are also many-faceted within yourself. Usually when you say 'I', the part you know, trust and with which you identify is speaking. When you explore yourself further you might find, either to your delight or consternation, that you are legion!

The Italian psychologist, Roberto Assagioli, formulated the system of self-analysis known as psychosynthesis (see Bibliography). He named the different aspects within, as 'subpersonalities'. Earlier C.G. Jung had spoken of the 'persona' or 'mask': your working or professional self, or persona, can be quite different from your relaxed, private or holiday self. You and those with whom you live and work need these masks. They help you to play the many different roles life may require of you.

In some ways the concept of the subpersonality goes further than that of the persona and refers to the deeper dynamics at work within your psyche. The persona is used more consciously. Your subpersonalities develop as a result of conditioning and can be survival mechanisms. They are distinctive energies within your being. To begin to identify these ask yourself the questions, 'What am I in bondage to?' and 'What makes my heart sing?'

Recognising your subpersonalities

You need to recognise and name some of your subpersonalities in order to work more closely with your soul, because if some inner aspects of your subpersonalities have autonomy in your behaviour patterns, your ability to see and discern the world beyond yourself can be limited. In psychology, projection happens when you project or see aspects of yourself mirrored, negatively, in others. If you project these things onto others, you might also project them onto your soul, so that you find it difficult to see your soul as a true friend and supporter. In working with your soul it is vital not to project onto it aspects such as the tyrant, the manipulator or the bully – all possible subpersonality themes (see the list below). If you find that you have a tendency to do this, then it is a good idea to go back to Exercise 1 (page 7) and revisit the vision of your soul as the beautiful chalice that holds the clear and non-consuming flame of your spirit.

Knowledge of subpersonalities helps you to know yourself better at a psychological level and therefore to know how to help yourself towards implementing both circumstantial and attitudinal change. Subpersonalities have themes such as power, authority, fear, attention to detail, survival and sabotage, and they can, to some extent, be taken through the interface area between transpersonal psychology and the field of esoteric spirituality. They can then be used to help you to bring insight into the archetypal themes given to you by your soul to work on in your present incarnation (see Chapter 7). Here are some common themes that subpersonalities represent:

- **The Hedonist** Lover of luxury and self-indulgence.
- **The Minimalist** Lover of frugality, with guilt about self-indulgence.
- **The Extrovert** Outgoing seeker of companions with perhaps a need to shine in, or organise social situations. This may be a subpersonality in someone who is otherwise more inward looking and introverted.

- **The Introvert** Inward looking, perhaps contemplative, maybe shy, not easily drawn out by others and might be a subpersonality in someone who is required for some reason to live more extrovertly.
- **The Victim** Not totally paranoid but feeling a sense of unfairness and victimisation in life and powerless to deal with:
- **The Tyrant** Dominating, seeking power over others, including **The Manipulator** and **The Bully** – probably needs to transform into **The Compassionate Leader.**
- **The Rescuer** Seeking to help others by providing them with solutions, particularly seeking to rescue the victim from The Tyrant – needs to transform into **The Enabler,** because he or she might become:
- **The Pseudo Martyr** Denies self in favour of others, but eventually builds resentment about what they are giving, because there is no equal return.
- **The Tidy Person** Abhors clutter, and can become a tyrant about it.
- **The Untidy Person** Disorganised and messy, can be related to The Saboteur.
- **The Manager** Related to **The Manipulator** or **The Controller,** needs to be in charge at all times.
- **The Parent** Wants to mother or father others and can be related to The Rescuer or The Pseudo Martyr).
- **The Inner Child** This is a subpersonality that can have many offshoots such as: **The Wounded Child, The Rebellious Child, The Naughty Child, The Secretive Child, The Hungry Child, The Eternal Child** or **The Golden Child.**
- **The Saboteur** may be fearful of success, and sabotages your self-image, holding you back from things you know you can do. This one can be very powerful, causing you to miss important interviews or appointments. If any of the other examples above are strong enough or not yet integrated they can also take on the power of The Saboteur.

Your *personal* subpersonalities

The above list is to some extent inexhaustible, because although subpersonalities have common themes they are also very personal to *you*. When you work with them and picture them imaginatively you may give them very individual names. For example my extrovert subpersonality is a Spanish dancer. My victim is a downtrodden woman with lanky hair and a mop and bucket always beside her. She is called 'Lily' as her image is reminiscent of a school cleaner I once met. There can be trouble between these two, when the Spanish dancer twirls past Lily with a supercilious expression, a flick of her frilled skirt and a click of her castanets.

Remember that subpersonalities are *aspects,* not caricatures, of yourself. To some extent they are distinct universes within you, and if they are not integrated into your central identity they may dominate your behaviour (become autonomous) particularly at times of stress. When integrated, you can use them as allies. To my usual rather shy and introverted self, my Spanish dancer can become a real ally at a party, even in the way I dress for such occasions.

The benefits of getting to know your subpersonalities

Time spent getting to know your subpersonalities can give you insight into any resistance to change you may have and can help you in either the process of making circumstantial change or that of making attitudinal change. Thinking about them flexibly and reflectively can also help you to identify themes you may be working with from lives that have gone before. You can find more information about subpersonalities and their relationship to spiritual and soul work in some of my other books, particularly *Working With Spirit Guides* (see Bibliography).

This chapter has aimed to set out and summarise seven of the main tools you can use to help you to gain a deeper understanding of your work with your soul and to encourage you to use these tools with positive awareness and purpose.

Exercises on using your inner worlds

The following exercises are intended to help you use your inner worlds to enable you to have a clearer or more direct communication with your soul.

Exercise 7 is a guided journey into your inner landscape, to help you have a sense of its layout and the inner scenery and landmarks you can encounter. Most transpersonal inner journeys start in a meadow, which is the transitional point at which you arrive as you enter the slightly altered state of consciousness that enables inner journeying. At any time in an inner journey where you may feel uncomfortable, (although this is unlikely), or feel that you have assimilated enough material for one occasion, you can return to your meadow and immediately back to an awareness of your breathing, your physical body and your outer world.

Exercise 7 helps to establish your inner landscape. Exercise 8 takes you back into your landscape but with a specific purpose of travelling to the point of higher awareness represented by the temple of your soul/higher self, where you can get a more direct sense of communication with your soul.

During both journeys I suggest that you meet up with a power animal and an inner wise being. If these are new concepts for you, you can look up their definition in the Glossary either before or after this inner journey, but on the whole I would suggest that you first trust the process and the experience. Intellectual definition can come later – or you may not need it at all. Before you begin, read through Preparing for the Exercises on page 5.

Exercise 7: *Mapping your inner landscape to find symbolic support and the potential for more direct communication with your soul*

Remember to have your special notebook or sheets of paper and crayons, pastels or paints to hand.

1. Make sure that you will be comfortable and undisturbed. Find your comfortable position.

2. Focus on the rhythm of your breathing. Be aware of each in-breath and out-breath, not trying to alter its tempo in any specific way, but allowing it to find its natural flow.

3. Sense your breath as coming in and out at the 'petals' of your heart centre or chakra (life energy centre). This lies in the centre of your body and aura on the same level as your physical heart (see Glossary).

4. As your regular breathing helps your heart chakra to open, get a sense of entering your own inner space or dimension.

5. Travel on your heart breath or energy into your inner landscape and find yourself in a meadow.

6. Activate all your inner senses so that you see the objects and colours, smell the fragrances, hear the sounds, touch the textures and savour the tastes.

7. Being in the meadow, take the opportunity to call to you a power animal to be your inner journeying companion. Your power animal may be any animal in existence, and although in the natural state of things it might be wild and

fierce, in your inner world it is your friend, protector and companion, and you feel comfortable with it and able to communicate with it.

8. Also take the opportunity to call to your inner wise being or presence. This may come to you as a being or person, or you may just sense a comforting and wise energy around you or perhaps a colour or fragrance that helps you to centre and feel in touch with your inner strength.

9. From your meadow, look out at the surrounding landscape. Nearby, there is a winding pathway that leads into a hilly area and you can see that it continues up into some mountains. The pathway leads to a plateau that is near the top of one of the mountains. As you look ahead you see that this plateau seems to be particularly alive and full of light, so that you feel very happy to be journeying there.

10. Call your inner wise presence and your power animal to join you on your journey and, looking around you as you go, make your way to the plateau, which is a vantage point over your landscape.

11. The path winds and the journey is surprisingly easy. Gradually, you are going upwards, but you can always see your meadow below and the attractive plateau ahead.

12. When you reach the plateau, take time to explore. You will probably find a source of clear, running, living water where you can refresh yourself. There may be a small sanctuary or travellers' rest for you to enter and explore. There will also be a place of natural sanctuary, with a sun-warmed rock against which to rest your back and look out over the landscape. Magically, there is a place where a rainbow light

shines. This is like the place of fairytales, where the rainbow meets the earth and bridges out beyond.

13. On this occasion be content to see this place where the rainbow bridge runs between your inner landscape and other planes and spheres. Do not step into the rainbow, or attempt to go any further than the plateau.

14. Remain in your chosen comfortable place and look at your inner landscape, noticing what it contains. At some point, which you can see from the plateau, the land meets the sea and there may be a lighthouse. In your landscape look for things such as a river, a forest, a rocky place, marshy land, a fertile plain, a rocky area with caves, a volcano, a desert area. Maybe there is a great tree of life, either in or near your forest. Outside one of the caves there may be a fire. Look for things that represent the four elements of earth, air, fire and water, and register the layout of your landscape so that you will have an idea of directions for future explorations.

15. Look out over your landscape from your comfortable place on the plateau for not more than 15 minutes (set a timer if you feel this necessary as a reminder). Know that having found and established this place in your inner landscape, you can always return to it, but now make your way back to the meadow, from which all these inner journeys begin and in which they end.

16. In the meadow, take leave of your power animal and your inner wise presence and then return to your awareness of your breath in your heart centre and so to the awareness of your breath in your body. Become conscious of the whole of your body and where you are sitting in your normal, everyday world. Feel your contact with the ground, open your eyes and connect with your outer surroundings, before

closing them again in order to visualise a cloak of light, with a hood, right around you.

17. Before you return to your everyday routines take the time to record this journey in your special notebook.

Exercise 8: journeying to the temple of your soul/higher self

This exercise starts in exactly the same way as Exercise 7 and then goes on to discover the temple of your soul, which is at the top of the mountain. For ease of use, I will repeat the instructions for the journey to the plateau and then add to them as you journey further. Have your special notebook or sheets of paper and crayons, pastels or paints to hand.

1. Make sure that you will be comfortable and undisturbed. Find your comfortable position

2. Focus on the rhythm of your breathing. Be aware of each in-breath and out-breath, not trying to alter its tempo in any specific way, but allowing it to find its natural flow.

3. Sense your breath as coming in and out at the 'petals' of your heart centre or chakra (life energy centre). This lies in the centre of your body and aura on the same level as your physical heart (see Glossary).

4. As your regular breathing helps your heart chakra to open, get a sense of entering your own inner space or dimension.

5. Travel on your heart breath or energy into your inner landscape and find yourself in a meadow.

6. Activate all your inner senses so that you see the objects and colours, smell the fragrances, hear the sounds, touch the textures and savour the tastes.

7. Being in the meadow, take the opportunity to call to you a power animal to be your inner journeying companion. Your power animal may be any animal in existence, and although in the natural state of things it might be wild and fierce, in your inner world it is your friend, protector and companion, and you feel comfortable with it and able to communicate with it.

8. Also take the opportunity to call to you your inner wise being or presence. This may come to you as a being or person, or you may just sense a comforting and wise energy around you or perhaps a colour or fragrance that helps you to centre and feel in touch with your inner strength.

9. From your meadow, look out at the surrounding landscape. Nearby, there is a winding pathway that leads into a hilly area and you can see that it continues up into some mountains. The pathway leads to a plateau that is near the top of one of the mountains. As you look ahead you see that this plateau seems to be particularly alive and full of light, so that you feel very happy to be journeying there.

10. Call your inner wise presence and your power animal to join you on your journey and, looking around you as you go, make your way to the plateau, which is a vantage point over your landscape.

11. The path winds and the journey is surprisingly easy. Gradually you are going upwards, but you can always see your meadow below and the attractive plateau ahead.

12. When you reach the plateau, take time to explore. You will probably find a source of clear, running, living water where you can refresh yourself and there may be a small sanctuary or travellers' rest for you to enter and explore. There will also be a place of natural sanctuary, with a sun-warmed rock against which to rest your back and look out over the landscape. Magically, there is a place where a rainbow light shines. This is like the place of fairytales, where the rainbow meets the earth and bridges out beyond.

13. On this occasion go near to the rainbow bridge, but do not step into it. Note that beside the rainbow bridge, there are some steps going upwards.

14. As you look at the steps and upwards, everything above you may seem a little misty, but also full of light.

15. You decide to climb the steps, taking your power animal and your inner wise presence with you. As you climb the steps you can see very clearly, even though when you look upwards the light-filled mist continues.

16. When you have climbed these steps, you see that above them the winding pathway continues and that ahead there is another set of steps. You climb the second set of steps and discover that beyond them the path winds once more and there is a third set of steps.

17. When you have climbed the third set of steps you realise that you have reached the outer courtyard of a temple of light, it glows particularly with violet, gold and white light, but there are other colours as well.

18. There is a pool ahead of you and intuitively you know that

you need to remove your shoes and walk through the pool. As you come to the far side there is a white robe laid out in readiness for you. You take off the clothes you are wearing and put the white robe on.

19. Your power animal lies down beside your clothes to wait for you; your inner wise presence continues to accompany you.

20. There is now a wide, flagged pathway to the door of the temple of light and you see that the door is standing open as if awaiting you, in welcome. You step inside, and hesitate a moment as you take in the light, sound, colour and fragrance here.

21. At the centre of the temple, which may be round, square or of another geometric design, there is a place to sit or kneel. You go to this place and realise that the ceiling at the centre of the temple is open, with a brilliant light of purple, white or gold pouring down upon you in healing and refreshment. This is the light of your soul.

22. Sit or kneel here, sensing contact with your soul and ask for blessing on the work you have been doing to make your relationship to your soul and its purposes more conscious. Ask to be helped in this awareness from this point onwards and for the light of your soul to shine clearly into any life dilemmas you are currently facing.

23. Stay here, accepting the light of your soul into every cell of your body for as long as you feel comfortable and then give thanks as you move away.

24. You may want to spend some time looking around the rest of the temple of your soul, or you may now be ready to

begin the journey back to your plateau and then to your meadow.

25. When you are ready to return, go through the door of the temple, back to the pool, where you rejoin your power animal, reclaim your clothes and shoes, and leave the temple robe behind you.

26. With your inner wise presence and your power animal beside you, make your way back down the three sets of steps and along the pathway that brings you down to the level of the plateau. Here you can refresh yourself again, from the source of living water before continuing downwards to your meadow, in your own time and at your own pace.

27. In the meadow take leave of your power animal and your inner wise presence and then return to your awareness of your breath in your heart centre and so to the awareness of your breath in your body.

28. Become conscious of the whole of your body and where you are sitting in your normal, everyday world. Feel your contact with the ground, open your eyes and connect with your outer surroundings, before closing them again in order to visualise a cloak of light, with a hood, right around you.

29. Before you return to your everyday routines take the time to record this journey in your special notebook.

Chapter 7 looks in depth at the place of archetypes as a tool in soul work and for enabling you to differentiate between soul work and soul service.

7

Archetypes as Tools for Soul Work and Soul Service

Having a knowledge of archetypes is a major tool in understanding the purposes of your soul and for coming to know more about what you are working out in your life. Archetypes, therefore, have a chapter to themselves. They can help you to recognise what guides and inspires you, give you insight into what may be challenging you and why, as well as helping you to differentiate between soul work (the whole of your life and the way you live it) and soul service (a call or will to follow a particular vocation such as teaching or nursing).

Archetypes

You may have met archetypes through the major arcana in Tarot cards. Of ancient origin, the Tarot pack has traditionally been used to help solve problems in life. The cards can also give you a clearer personal and individual understanding of the purposes of your soul and where you stand in your soul journey. When well read by an experienced Tarot reader, they can be a valuable instrument for decoding soul wisdom and direction.

The major arcana of a Tarot pack consists of 22 archetypal images that depict the challenges, signs and major stages of human experience and evolution. The Tarot archetypes are personified as: The Fool; The Magician; The High Priestess; The Empress; The

Emperor; The Hierophant; The Lovers; The Chariot; Strength; The Hermit; The Wheel of Fortune; Justice; The Hanged Man; Death; Temperance; The Devil; The Tower; The Star; The Moon; The Sun; Judgement; The World.

These 22 personified images aim to illustrate the total evolutionary journey of your soul. At some time in the journey of evolution, each of these figures or situations, with the deep symbolic meaning behind them, will have to be met and dealt with.

In the Tarot, the archetypes are personified though the forces that affect each human society and can also be named as more abstract principles such as love, justice, peace, beauty, purity, harmony, power, service, wholeness, wisdom, healing and perfection. To personify these is to degrade them. Thus the illustrated and personified archetypal images of the Tarot come from purer archetypal principles that have been degraded in order to make them more accessible and understandable.

Archetypes, whether pure or degraded, affect you as an individual as well as each society. Individuals and societies struggle to live by the archetypes of the higher qualities listed above and use them in deciding what is 'good' and 'right' or what is 'bad' and 'wrong'.

A consideration of archetypes can give you a fuller comprehension of your life aims, drives and blockages, and give you insight into your soul work as well as your soul service. One way of looking at the evolution of the soul is to see it as a process whereby you learn about the shadow side as well as the bright side of each of the great archetypal principles. Can you truly know what peace is, unless you have known war or strife? Do you appreciate justice unless you have seen or experienced the effects of injustice? Can you work in true consciousness of the positive aspects without experiencing the negative? Is it possible to know what you want without knowing what you do not want?

Messages from your soul: themes that challenge

Many of the themes that will challenge you in life, and therefore signal that there is soul work to be addressed, are archetypal in nature. These themes are put on your pathway by your soul, as part of its need to embrace as wide an experience as possible in order to evolve. In their challenging mode, the archetypal themes will be related to the shadow or darker side of the archetypes or to confrontations with the archetypal principles. Identifying your challenging archetypes can help you to a deeper understanding and decoding of your soul contract as well as aiding your sense of what has gone before in the experience of your soul.

The following is a list of how the archetypes of higher qualities might confront you in your daily living of life:

- **Love** Being confronted by Love might mean that you find it difficult to feel loved or to find satisfying relationships.
- **Justice** Challenges in the area of Justice might mean that you have to deal with personal or collective *injustice*. Your life might involve having to expend time and energy in dealing with legal proceedings.
- **Peace** Being under the shadow side of the archetype of Peace might mean that you are often involved in disputes, or maybe have to adjudicate in them. It could also mean that the area where you live is an area where war is being waged and that you have to suffer all the privations, dangers and fears that being in such a place might bring.
- **Beauty** If Beauty is your testing area, then it might be that you are concerned about your own physical appearance, or that your surroundings are of the man-made variety where there is no natural beauty, no clean air and nothing to inspire you in the environment.
- **Purity** The darker side of Purity might mean that you are confronted with environmental pollution or that you long for clarity of mind. You might be challenged to make compromises,

and feel that they are anathema to you. Perhaps you might be passionate about belief or religion and frustrated by what you see as the confusion or lack of one-pointedness in others. You might, in pursuing a strong religious or ideological belief, feel that others alienate you or discriminate against you.

- **Harmony** The confrontations of the prickly side of the archetype of Harmony might be experienced in many different areas of life, perhaps in family life, other relationships, or work situations. It could even be that you long to be able to sing or play an instrument but are unable to do so, because of either lack of opportunity or talent.

- **Power** The archetype of Power and its shadow side effects most people in one way or another. We all have to deal with authority and find the right attitudes towards the establishment. We have to learn not to let others have inappropriate power over us or to 'give away our power'. We have to find our own inner authority in order to take full responsibility for our lives and decisions. To be afflicted by the archetype of power may mean that you experience loss of freedom or that you have to wield power in a difficult situation.

- **Service** Dealing with the shadow side of Service might mean that you have a compulsion or an obsession about service. It might mean that you work in a job to which you are tied or feel almost enslaved by, seemingly with no opportunity for escape (see also Martin's story, page 85).

- **Wholeness** To be dealing with the afflicted side of the archetype of Wholeness might mean that in some way your body is not whole, that you are frequently ill or carry a chronic sickness or disabling condition. It might mean that you are mentally ill and feel fragmented. It could also mean that your family of origin or your later family by marriage is dysfunctional, not whole, and yet you yearn for wholeness and healing.

- **Healing** The shadow side of the archetype of Healing may also mean that you have some life-long condition, perhaps from birth, that you struggle to find healing for. It might mean that a loved one needs healing and you cannot find it for them.

- **Perfection** The flip side of the archetype of Perfection could mean that you are a perfectionist who sits unhappily in your skin because you cannot achieve the perfection you seek. Others may have sought to mould you to their standards of perfection so that your true self has gone unrecognised and feels shackled and imprisoned.

- **Wisdom** The shadow side of the archetype of Wisdom might mean that you felt yourself to be the victim of biased or unwise advice or had a tendency to leap into things without considering consequences. It might also mean that you unwittingly set causes in action without consideration for the effects and the reverberations not only on others but also back to yourself.

These negative sides and effects of the archetypes link directly with the list of themes that challenge, already given in Chapter 4: power; love; relationships; wealth; poverty; body; sexuality; religion and belief; control; health; social position; possessions; fears; feeling displaced; image; acceptance; rejection; expectation; wounding; victimhood; dilemmas of action and inaction; choice; authority; the search for approval.

Whatever theme(s) you identify, if you are dealing with them at the retributive level of soul work, you may just have to make up your mind to bear with them until a way out is found. You may need to trust that when the time is right you will be able to make a breakthrough to either attitudinal or circumstantial change or that there will be a release through synchronicity.

If you are dealing with them at the redemptive level of karma, then you might be working to help yourself and others overcome the effects of the shadow side of the archetypal themes or you may be very aware of needing to seek or restore a balance in certain areas. If you are at the transcendent stage, you may recognise that you have met certain challenging themes in your life but have worked through any hold that these themes may have had for you. Identifying the themes will open up the opportunity to see where you are in your soul work with them and to feel the sense of reason, purpose, meaning and soul intention for them being there for you to deal with.

Messages from your soul: gifts that inspire

If the themes that challenge are linked to the shadow side of the archetypes of higher qualities; then the gifts that inspire you and that you use to inspire others are linked to the bright side of those archetypes. Gifts can also be part of your retributive and redemptive soul work if you have to struggle in order to get your gifts or talents recognised. In that struggle there will be a learning process.

You might be a gifted individual who has had your gifts and talents recognised from an early age and have been given opportunities to be appropriately trained and so realise your potential. At the right time you may have found wider acknowledgement so that your pathway to success and fulfilment seemed blessed and easily assured.

You might, on the other hand, have always known that you had a gift, but been forced by circumstances, or by parents and teachers who thought that they were working in your best interests, to use your talent at best as a hobby rather than being encouraged to develop it in a mainstream way.

Again, your gift might have been recognised but the gateways to training it might have been closed, so that you were left only with a dream. You might, because of any of the above reasons, have to work very hard to realise your dream, or you might opt for the attitudinal change that enables you to relate to a dream that is unlikely to come to fruition, either because of intransigent lack of opportunity or through choice involving sacrifice. One of the most testing times for relationship to working with your soul is when accidents happen that prevent the development of a gift or suddenly halt a burgeoning and fulfilling career.

Your innate gifts can give you new insights into working with your soul and perhaps particularly add clarity to any thoughts you might be having about what has gone before. If you find it difficult to bring your gift to fruition, then maybe a past personality bead has either not respected giftedness enough or has used it vainly or for reasons of power or hedonism. If something that seems to be blossoming well is suddenly snatched from you, then perhaps previously a past incarnate bead from your soul thread took too much for granted or was drawn into a life of tunnel vision, narrowed by too much focus on the gift and nothing but the gift.

How the archetypes of higher qualities inspire

In contrast to the themes that can be linked to the shadow side of the archetypes of higher qualities are the main attributes and areas of inspiration covered by their bright side.

- **Love** The archetype of Love is connected to: love of God, love of others, love of selfless sacrifice, heroism, tenderness, mothering, nurturing, caring, creativity, dedication, vocation, commitment, healing, love of earth and growing things, love of animals, conservation, transformation and giving contentment.

- **Justice** The archetype of Justice is connected to: fairness, administration, law, order, guardianship, authority, leadership, reform, social conscience, politics, mitigation, arbitration, warriorship, human rights, debate, caring, idealism, advocacy and compassion.

- **Peace** The archetype of Peace is connected to: peace-making, warriorship, arbitration, citizenship, defence, guardianship, healing, planning, order, freedom, relating, union, humanitarianism, safety, prayer, meditation and quietude.

- **Beauty** The archetype of Beauty is connected to: preservation, creativity, shaping, artistry, skill, observation, grace, transformation, appreciation, colour, design, architecture, building, vision, assessment, perspective and awareness.

- **Purity** The archetype of Purity is connected to: one-pointedness, clear vision, planning, conservation, art, idealism, integrity and vision for the potential of humanity.

- **Harmony** The archetype of Harmony is connected to: music, creativity, peace-making, dance, art, colour, design, symmetry, arbitration, counselling, inner searching, healing, friendship, empathy, rhythm, understanding and tolerance.

- **Power** The archetype of Power is connected to rulership, leadership, teaching, priesthood, government, self-empowerment, empowerment of others, ambition, initiating, competitiveness, acquisition, responsibility, direction, inspiration, vision, hope, dedication, idealism, belief, courage, confidence, law and order, competence.

- **Service** The archetype of Service is connected to: dedication, purpose, serving others, service of religion, pastoral care, vision for humanity, responsibility, administration, law and order, transformation, transmutation, healing, counselling, giving, self-sacrifice, social conscience, belief, social reform, improvement, idealism, patriotism, humanitarianism and love of others.

- **Wholeness** The archetype of Wholeness is connected to self-growth, equality, balance, inclusiveness, healing, perception, blending, acceptance, seeking, exploration, assimilation, completion, vision, tolerance, breadth of knowledge, making the dysfunctional functional, human potential, symbolism and creativity.

- **Healing** The archetype of Healing is connected to healing of all kinds, collective health, human potential, functioning to the highest potential, enabling individuals, enabling the evolution of humanity, creative relationship, relationships between species, and defining health.

- **Perfection** The archetype of Perfection is connected to idealism, God, consciousness, dedication, striving, healing, endeavour, vision, stoicism, industriousness, seeking the highest, goodness, belief, setting standards, aims, goal setting, confidence, focus, advising, leadership, artistry, worth, conservation, preservation, following a prescribed path closely, application and diligence.

- **Wisdom** The archetype of Wisdom is connected to art, depth of knowledge, compassion, justice, teaching, leadership, interpretation of knowledge and celebration of difference.

Soul work and soul service

Having a knowledge of the archetypes will help you distinguish between soul work and soul service. Making this differentiation is important because if you have found a vocation or absorbing career in life you may feel that giving yourself to this in a dedicated way is all that working with your soul is about. For many people, there is a definable soul service that your soul wants you to do in the world, but for equally as many there is not. Even if you know what you have to do in life and do it with passion and fulfilment, serving the community *and* your soul, there will still be work to do on yourself, as a conscious and sentient being, living the everyday business of life and bringing meaning to *that* as well. Bringing meaning to what may sometimes seem to be the minutiae of life is what soul *work* is mostly about.

When you see working with your soul as the art of managing life at every moment, you may realise that you have already been doing it without naming it. Every time you dig your way out of a hole, take stock of your life and decide it needs to change, or look for ways of dealing with obstacles and challenges in as harmonious a way as possible, you are working with your soul.

Soul *service* is what many people seek. As stated earlier, the most common question I hear in either psychotherapy or channelling is, 'What am I *meant* to be doing?' There is an assumption in this question that something other than yourself has a plan for your life but is keeping it shrouded in mystery and that if you could only know what the plan is then life would become clear and simple. There is an implication in the word 'meant' that there is no choice. When this question is put to Gildas, he often says that what you are *meant* to be doing is exactly what you *are* doing, until *you* choose to change it. If you are in a dilemma about where to take the pathway of your life, then you are storing for your soul the experience of what it is like to be in that dilemma, and this will be one of your offerings to your soul thread when you return to it with your 'traveller's tales'. Learning to put your house in order on a very mundane level is a major concern of life and is perhaps one of the best definitions of soul work. Another might be 'learning to be comfortable in your own skin'.

If you have defined or been drawn to a specific, nameable work in life and are getting on with it, then you are serving your soul and perhaps your soul group (see Chapter 2). On one level at least you are probably able to say that you know where you are going in life.

Soul service has a connection with the givens of your life (see Chapter 4) and with that in which you are gifted or talented, or for which you have discovered a passion. You will want to offer what you have to those who have need of it or who will be served, helped or enthused by it. You may find that developing what you have and working with it is either a welcome or an inescapable destiny.

Destiny and free choice

To some extent, I see my work with Gildas as both a welcome privilege *and* an inescapable destiny. I believe that, despite the work your soul lays down for you, you still have a lot of free choice in your life. My dilemma is not so much that it would not be possible to choose not to do my work with Gildas but that having built the relationship with him and developed the work together, I would no longer feel whole without either him or the work. There is no other work I would rather do and I have had the privilege of building it in a way that gives me flexibility *and* a lifestyle. I have been granted an enormous amount of synchronicity in my life, and although I do not tend to ask questions of Gildas in the same way as our clients do, I always feel a tremendous amount of support and protection from him and the spheres from which he comes. So, if it is a destiny, it is a happy one.

I also, of course, have a normal life beyond my work with Gildas. I am very aware that my work with him is inspired and that many synchronicities have happened to determine its direction. In my normal life I am much more 'on my own'. Much of my soul work in former years has lain in the dilemmas of being a single parent. It has been about how to make a life of my own as well as being a channel for Gildas. It is currently concerned with the process of ageing and trying to grow old gracefully – and sometimes outrageously – but always with endeavouring to cultivate a sense of soulful cooperation.

Decoding your soul contract

You may not have a nameable destiny or calling but you do have a soul contract that combines destiny in a lower-key sense as well as free choice. Soul work is about endeavouring to decode that soul contract, to accept both its limitations and its opportunities and to learn to make the choices that can give you joy in living and enable you to celebrate your place in the world.

Gildas teaches that if you look at things in the right way, 'you are always in the right place at the right time, wherever that may be'. At first sight that might seem like a comforting teaching but, thinking of some places we can get ourselves into, it is also extremely challenging. Once again, it all comes down to the way in which you determine to handle your life and the power you claim or cultivate to make change where it is required.

You *can* only work with your soul from where you are at any given moment, and working with your soul means working to make yourself thrive and to have joy, satisfaction or meaning in your life. So, although you may wish for soul service and clarity about what you are 'meant' to be doing, it is by no means always forthcoming. Working with your soul is connected to putting what has to be done in each moment into a context that brings you meaning. It is not good to put your life on hold, because you are constantly searching for the thing you are 'meant' to be doing without finding it. It is *your* life and you have the privilege of creating it within the parameters laid down by your soul's initial life choices or givens.

Working with your soul can also include *creating* your soul service, if life has not made it clear to you.

Creating your soul service

It is in considering how you have created – or how you intend to create – your soul service that the archetypes of higher qualities can be of aid to you. Ponder on the archetypes of higher qualities and the key areas they will inspire, as I have suggested, and consider which of these stir or move you.

We are a *doing* orientated society, but not all soul service connects to this attitude. You must take care to ensure that you also consider the key words in relationship to lifestyles that are potentially more *being* orientated. Creating and maintaining a beautiful home or garden, or mothering, are at one level very active and demanding tasks, yet it is the happy home-maker's quality of being that touches others. You may also realise that the actual nature of the work you do is less important than the quality of being you are able to bring to it. It is possible to learn to *be* through *doing* and to *do* through *being*.

Because the archetypes of higher qualities have a complex inter-relationship they cannot be simplistically separated from each other. A life connected to the archetype of Service may also be causing you to work with your soul on Wholeness, Justice or Love, and vice versa. If you are over-dedicated to one particular archetype, or even obsessive about it, you may unconsciously create imbalances in your ability to honour some of the others. Such imbalances set causes in action and produce effects that may lead to more work for you and your soul, either in this present lifetime or to pass on to the future incarnation of another personality bead from your soul thread.

Sarah's accident, as explained in her story below, could be seen as part of her destiny. Her soul chose a very dramatic way in which to present her with her ambassadorial work. She came through a dark time with flying colours and was able to turn what could have been tragedy into psychological advantage. Sarah agreed to the use of her story here even though, as far as she is concerned, it is being used to illustrate an unfamiliar context and angle of understanding. During the long time of her rehabilitation, she felt that something other than her many friends, helpers and therapists was giving her strength. She also said that within the whole experience there was a sense of something inevitable and that from early on in her awareness her life would never be the same again, she knew that she was going to be able to take charge again and would not become a victim. Her story is one of the marriage between a (severe) knock on the head of a somewhat rough destiny and the creative free will that can find the gold beyond the dross.

Sarah's story

Sarah had been brought up on a farm. From an early age she had been taught to ride and there were always horses around. She was a natural in the saddle, and a friend of her father's seeing her riding on her pony when she was about ten years old encouraged Sarah's parents to let her have the training that would develop her skills. As her talent was recognised by others, so her parents invested in the best horses possible to complement her expertise. She was gradually acknowledged as a very gifted young rider in the eventing world and tipped as a hope for the Olympics. It was not to be, however. In a riding accident, Sarah broke her spine and became paraplegic. There was widespread shock and devastation at her plight and it took a long time for Sarah to gain any independence in life again and for those who loved her and who had gloried in seeing her shine, to get over their shock and grief. During her recovery period, Sarah displayed enormous courage and surmounted many hurdles earlier than expected and even some that she had not been expected to overcome. The courage that had made her such a flourishing horsewoman was now displayed in her determination to reach the fullest potential possible within her physical limitations. She was still passionate about horses and riding. She did not ever actually sit on a horse herself again, but eventually, after many struggles, she was able to take part in instructing young riders and also in schemes for riding for the disabled and horse rescue work. She did not, and of course, could not, in the circumstances, say that the accident was the best thing that had ever happened to her, but she did feel that her life had taken on a greater depth because of it. Before the accident she was set to shine, possibly for her country. She had loved the world of competition and training but felt that in overcoming her accident she had discovered inner strengths and reserves she had not known she possessed. Sarah also felt that the work she was now doing was healing and she was inspired as much by the individuals she had contact with as they were inspired by her.

Exercise on reviewing the archetypal qualities

The following exercise, which is in two parts, offers the opportunity for a reflective review of both the shadow and bright side of the archetypal qualities. It is presented as a means of getting further perspective on your work with your soul. It can also help you to see more clearly what your soul service might be and in creating that aspect of your life if it is not yet evident and clear. The reflective review is followed by another opportunity to use Exercise 8, Journeying to the Temple of Your Soul/Higher Self (page 99), to ask your soul to give you a clearer perception of the archetypes that are of importance in your present soul contract. Before you begin, read through Preparing for the Exercises on page 5.

Exercise 9: *pondering the archetypal input that gives you insight into working with your soul and your soul service*

Part 1
This is an informal reflective exercise and is not designed to be contained within a certain time space. If you think about this regularly, even at the back of your mind, over a period of days or weeks it will help you to recognise more about the input of your soul's inclusion of archetypal themes into your soul contract.

Begin by reading through again the parts of this chapter that list the ways in which both the shadow and bright side of the archetypes of higher qualities can give you life themes that challenge and life themes that inspire (pages 106–112). Use your special notebook to note down anything that is said in these sections that you feel particularly applies to you.

Although I have given the exercise a formal format, remember that this is not a process that can be finished at one sitting. You are aiming to set a process in motion, and insights will continue to come through as long as you are intent on understanding more about your soul contract and working with your soul. If your special notebook is kept in an accessible place, you can note these down as they make themselves known. You can also repeat the formal exercise on a number of occasions.

Each time you take the formal approach to this exercise, read through the reflections and life reviews you have accumulated as a result of the previous exercises.

1. Make sure that you will be comfortable and undisturbed. Find your comfortable position

2. Focus on the rhythm of your breathing. Be aware of each in-breath and out-breath, not trying to alter its tempo in any specific way, but allowing it to find its natural flow.

3. Sense your breath as coming in and out at the 'petals' of your heart centre or chakra (life energy centre). This lies in the centre of your body and aura on the same level as your physical heart (see Glossary).

4. As your regular breathing helps your heart chakra to open, get a sense of entering your own inner space or dimension.

5. In this relaxed state, and having read the material you have

noted from previous exercises, centre on the qualities of the shadow and bright side of the archetypes of higher principles, especially any you may have made a note of as you re-read and re-considered them. Look at your checklist from time to time if you wish to do so.

6. Make some notes on your present reflections. Write additional key words as well as more wordy descriptions. You might want to write words in different colours or use colour to draw patterns as you reflect on the material.

7. When you have spent between 20 and 30 minutes in this heart-centred, heart-breathing state, close your notebook or put your paper aside, feel your feet firmly on the ground, become aware of your everyday surroundings, walk around a little, make yourself a drink, step outside and breathe fresh air, or do something else that is practical and grounding, bringing you firmly back into your present everyday world.

8. Now, or later, you may want to open your notebook or look at your papers again and contemplate what you have written and noted in this exercise.

Part 2

This part of the exercise is similar to Exercise 8 where you took a guided inner journey to the temple of your soul/higher self. The beginning is exactly the same as Exercise 8 but for ease of reference I will repeat the instructions here. The difference lies in the task or question you are taking to the temple of your soul/higher self. You are making the journey this time to ask your soul to bring you clarity about the archetypes it has included in your soul contract for you to work with. Have your special notebook or sheets of paper and crayons, pastels or paints to hand.

1. Make sure that you will be comfortable and undisturbed. Find your comfortable position

2. Focus on the rhythm of your breathing. Be aware of each in-breath and out-breath, not trying to alter its tempo in any specific way, but allowing it to find its natural flow.

3. Sense your breath as coming in and out at the 'petals' of your heart centre or chakra (life energy centre). This lies in the centre of your body and aura on the same level as your physical heart (see Glossary).

4. As your regular breathing helps your heart chakra to open, get a sense of entering your own inner space or dimension.

5. Travel on your heart breath or energy into your inner land-scape and find yourself in a meadow.

6. Activate all your inner senses so that you see the objects and colours, smell the fragrances, hear the sounds, touch the textures and savour the tastes.

7. Being in the meadow, take the opportunity to call to you a power animal to be your inner journeying companion. Your power animal may be any animal in existence, and although in the natural state of things it might be wild and fierce, in your inner world it is your friend, protector and companion, and you feel comfortable with it and able to communicate with it.

8. Also take the opportunity to call to you your inner wise being or presence. This may come to you as a being or person, or you may just sense a comforting and wise energy around you or perhaps a colour or fragrance that helps you to centre and feel in touch with your inner strength.

9. From your meadow, look out at the surrounding landscape. Nearby, there is a winding pathway that leads into a hilly area and you can see that it continues up into some mountains. The pathway leads to a plateau that is near the top of one of the mountains. As you look ahead you see that this plateau seems to be particularly alive and full of light, so that you feel very happy to be journeying there.

10. Call your inner wise presence and your power animal to join you on your journey and, looking around you as you go, make your way to the plateau, which is a vantage point over your landscape.

11. The path winds and the journey is surprisingly easy. Gradually you are going upwards, but you can always see your meadow below and the attractive plateau ahead.

12. When you reach the plateau, take time to explore. You will probably find a source of clear running, living water, where you can refresh yourself, and there may be a small sanctuary or travellers' rest for you to enter and explore. There will also be a place of natural sanctuary, with a sun-warmed rock against which to rest your back and look out over the landscape. Magically, there is a place where a rainbow light shines. This is like the place of fairytales, where the rainbow meets the earth and bridges out beyond.

13. On this occasion go near to the rainbow bridge, but do not step into it. Note that beside the rainbow bridge, there are some steps going upwards.

14. As you look at the steps and upwards, everything above you may seem a little misty, but also full of light.

15. You decide to climb the steps, taking your power animal and your inner wise presence with you. As you climb the steps you can see very clearly, even though when you look upwards the light-filled mist continues.

16. When you have climbed these steps, you see that above them the winding pathway continues and that ahead there is another set of steps. You climb the second set of steps and discover that beyond them is a winding path again and a third set of steps.

17. When you have climbed the third set of steps you realise that you have reached the outer courtyard of a temple of light, it glows particularly with violet, gold and white light, but there are other colours as well.

18. There is a pool ahead of you and intuitively you know that you need to remove your shoes and walk through the pool. As you come to the far side of the pool there is a white robe laid out in readiness for you. You take off the clothes you are wearing and put the white robe on.

19. Your power animal lies down beside your clothes to wait for you, but your inner wise presence continues to accompany you.

20. There is now a wide, flagged pathway to the door of the temple of light and you see that the door is standing open as if awaiting you, in welcome. You step inside, and hesitate a moment as you take in the light, sound, colour and fragrance here.

21. At the centre of the temple, which may be round, square or of another geometric design, there is a place to sit or kneel.

You go to this place and realise that the ceiling at the centre of this temple is open, with a brilliant light of purple, white or gold pouring down upon you in healing and refreshment. This is the light of your soul. Feel it expanding around you like a cloak of golden light. Let the light penetrate each part, each cell of your body, bringing you warmth, light, healing and inspiration.

22. Within the blessing of the light of your soul, reflectively consider the archetypes of higher qualities and the thoughts you have had about them. Open your eyes, briefly, if you need to do so, in order to check your notes.

23. Consider the things in your life that might be described as themes that challenge (spend about 3-5 minutes on this).

24. Consider the things in your life that feed your creativity and sense of fulfilment.

25. Ask yourself what you feel may be missing from your life. Ask that any words or symbols that will enable you to be clearer about your sense of purpose or soul contract in your present lifetime may come clearly into your mind (spend about 5-10 minutes on this).

26. Stay here, for a few more moments, accepting the light of your soul into every cell of your body, and asking it to help you find the clarity you might need for working with your soul. After 3-5 minutes, give thanks and move away.

27. When you are ready to return, go through the door of the temple, back to the pool, where you rejoin your power animal, reclaim your clothes and shoes, and leave the temple robe behind you.

28. With your inner wise presence and your power animal beside you, make your way back down the three sets of steps and along the pathway that brings you down to the level of the plateau. Here you can refresh yourself again, from the source of living water before continuing downwards to your meadow, in your own time and at your own pace.

29. In the meadow take leave of your power animal and your inner wise presence and then return to your awareness of your breath in your heart centre and so to the awareness of your breath in your body.

30. Become conscious of the whole of your body and where you are sitting in your normal, everyday world. Feel your contact with the ground, open your eyes and connect with your outer surroundings, before closing them again in order to visualise a cloak of light, with a hood, right around you.

31. Before you return to your everyday routines take the time to record this journey in your special notebook.

Chapter 8 considers illness and dark nights of the soul as an integral part of the journey.

8

Illness and Dark Nights of the Soul

Your soul places you in calculated and specific situations for your incarnation. It puts you through the stages of retributive, redemptive and transcendent soul work (see Chapter 3). It might then seem that your soul is the main conditioning or grooming influence in your life intent on shaping you for its own purposes. To some extent this is true. Your experience of life, whatever it may be, awakens you. It is your soul's intention that you discover your power to tackle or change your quality of life and your overall life direction. Experiencing contentment and support in life makes you seek to maintain that. Experiencing unease or dis-ease with the way in which your life seems to be unfolding can motivate and inspire you to seek and make changes, to try things and take calculated risks that otherwise you might not have considered.

Your core self and your conditioned self

As you become conscious of how you want to shape your life, so you begin to get in touch with your core or true self. Knowing what you don't want or enjoy, what frustrates you and does not fulfil you, is part of the journey towards knowing what you *do* want and the price you are willing to pay to make sure you get it. Trials, challenges and frustrations may be part of your retributive soul work, but once you sense that, whatever they may be, there is a power within you that can bring about either attitudinal or circumstantial change (see Chapters 3 and 6), you are well on your way to stepping into the personally more rewarding phase of redemptive soul work.

When the voice of your core is heard

Opposition may often depress and frustrate. It can make you feel powerless, at least temporarily. On the other hand it can also give you the fire energy necessary for making a more creative relationship with it. When this happens you begin to consider what *you* actually want from your life rather than endeavouring to conform to what other people or other influences seem to expect of you.

We have seen how much of the basic shape or initial clauses of your soul contract can be understood or decoded from the choices that you have made about where and with whom your incarnation begins. Your soul has an agenda and makes you its messenger or ambassador for that agenda. By living with and through the givens of your life you have the opportunity to gain awareness and to come to conclusions about how you might want your life to change. When you are uneasy with your lot and determine to seek change, this is the time when the voice of your true, or core, self begins to make itself heard.

Your soul is both clever and wise, it sets an agenda of soul work, but the ultimate achievement in which it will rejoice with you is when you discover and work to bring to fruition all the things that make your heart sing. When you take the courage to shape your own life without undue reference to the expectations of others you can be sure that you are working with your soul. Its primary aim is to help you to be faithful to your core, true or blueprint self, knowing that when you achieve such an alignment you will live with that abundant joy and health that enables you to *know* that you are at one with both spirit and soul. It is a joyful and creative living that sometimes shines through very difficult circumstances. That is the greatest gift you can give not only to yourself and your soul but also to the collective of humanity.

Evolution leads to wholeness and there can be no wholeness

without integrity. Recognising and noting the points in life where you feel that you have acted, reacted, interacted or made a choice that you know comes from an inner point of integrity helps you recognise what it means to be in touch with your core self. Following the exercises given throughout this book will help you to make these recognitions.

The soul's investment: revealing your core self

As well as making you an ambassador for its own evolution, the tests and dilemmas your soul causes you to face in life can only be finally and successfully addressed when you act from that inner place of integrity that is the attribute of your core self. The tests are partly there to help you find that aspect of yourself. Your soul seeks not to *condition* but to *enable* you to express your true self.

Awakening to recognise your core self can be similar to a mystical experience. Exercise 1 (page 7) aims to help you to hold a vision of the mysterious and mystical unity between soul and spirit. Although it is not to be expected that you will at all times be in touch with your core self, the moments when it happens are similar to the soul, holding within its clear chalice the living but non-consuming flame of your spirit. The image or experience sought in Exercise 1 is at one and the same time the symbol for how it feels to be working, living and choosing from the integrity of your core self. Exercise 10 on page 149 of this chapter will also help you to feel a sense of what this aspect of working with your soul is all about.

All of the individuals whose stories are featured in these chapters encountered serious life dilemmas, but found courageous solutions. These accounts do not have all the ingredients of the traditional and-they-lived-happily-ever-after stories, yet in another sense the subjects of all these case histories *did* live happily ever after. That happiness came from having dug deep into their inner reserves in order to come through a testing experience. In each case the core self was touched and the resolution resonated so successfully only because it sprung from core self integrity.

The experience of such solutions has a transcendent quality that is not subject to 'if only's'. It brings an implicit sense of having acquired serious life tools and completed a good piece of ambassadorial work with the full cooperation and approval of soul and spirit.

The effects of others' expectations

Your soul puts you on the pathway to honing your true self, but life conditions you in what may often be, in terms of soul work, a rather dangerous way. The expectations imposed on you, by parents, the establishment, society, and eventually by yourself, may cause you stress, but all too often, at least for a part of your life, you will try to please and conform. The tendency is 'to give yourself a good talking to', take a deep breath, call on your willpower and then carry on pursuing aims, objectives and patterns that more often than not are those that you have been expected or conditioned to follow and which are not necessarily those of your core self. Too many people put up with being a round peg in a square hole for too long before they endeavour to change either the peg or the hole.

Parents, teachers and society have an investment in moulding or forcing you into conformity not because they do not love you or care about your future welfare, but sometimes because they love or care too much. In general they want you to be successful, fulfilled and solvent. They therefore push you towards training for secure jobs and developing the skills that society most needs at any given time in order that you will be able to get onto the housing ladder, to save sensibly for your future and generally to be seen, in worldly terms, to be 'doing well'.

Such things do, of course, have an indisputable value, but sometimes the creative person wants to approach them by more indirect routes. One of my clients, Samantha, came for counselling and support when her parents were angry with her because she did not want to join the family business. When she insisted, instead, on fulfilling a personal dream and working to put herself through medical school she spent some years maintaining only a difficult and often tenuous relationship with her family. Eventually, when she finished the long training and got her first hospital job, her family were almost overawed at her achievements and her title of Dr. The journey to breakthrough had not been easy for all concerned.

They have their reasons

My own parents, having already faced the privations of the First World War, married and became parents to my brother and myself as the Second World War was raging. They were intelligent people, but my father had left school aged 12 years and my mother at 13 years. They had immediately gone into full-time work in very mundane jobs: my father worked on a conveyor belt sticking labels on paint tins and my mother slaved at a sewing machine in what she called 'a making-up firm'. They both managed to educate themselves later and move into professional work: my mother as a nurse and my father as a youth worker. It was small wonder that their dream for myself was that I should become a teacher, preferably progressing to a head teacher, and that my brother should work in a bank, with the potential of becoming a manager. At that time, those jobs were known for their security and for the pensions guaranteed at the end of a fixed number of years of service.

My brother and I protested that we were not interested in doing these jobs, but we were considered too young and too irresponsible to know what we were talking about. At that time, there was less potential to rebel seriously against parents' directives and our protests were ineffective. According to our parents' wishes I went into teacher training and my brother moved on from school into banking. My parents thought they were doing the very best for us and that as far as they were concerned our lives were all set to become dreams come true. I am sure that they had little recognition that it was their own dreams that they were asking us to live out.

Seeking others' approval

Thus you might find yourself pressurised into pursuing interests seen by others as being 'good' for you. You are expected to perform to a preset standard and generally become happy, normal or well adjusted. Your mind learns to believe that these norms or expectations are right. You may turn yourself inside out in order to please others and fulfil their ambitions for you. There are few who cannot be seduced by the common human yearning for approval.

In today's world, it seems that a balance of power is in the process of taking effect. To some extent the pendulum has perhaps swung too far in the opposite direction. Parents do not have an easy time if they try to push their offspring into conformity. The lowering of the age of consent from 21 years old to 18 years old has certainly had something to do with this. I was teaching my first class of young children while I was still technically a minor. I remember how bizarre it seemed that I had to get my parents' permission in order to have a polio jab on an occasion when it was recommended that all teachers should do so. Although I had never wanted to teach in the established educational system, I could still see, and to some extent appreciate, where my parents were coming from. In the event, having such a career, did, in many practical ways, serve me well. In those times parents handed down tried-and-trusted values in what they sincerely believed to be our best interests.

The image makers

There is, however, other very powerful conditioning in the world of today. Image makers and spin doctors have enormous sway. They often earn or accumulate huge sums of money for what they do. They put great energy into selling their ideas or products and into brainwashing individuals into a desire to acquire either material objects or a certain style in order to have all eyes turned upon us because of the 'cool' or 'trendy' way we act or look. You probably despised your school uniform, but soon after you were no longer required to wear it, became only too anxious to acquire the clothes that are little more than uniforms, cleverly sold by those who are supposed to know what helps you to get ahead.

Because these influences are so powerful, they have affected judgements so much and swung values to their own advantage; the sad thing is that they have managed to create a society in which they *do* know, if you move in certain worlds, exactly how to 'help' you get ahead by subscribing to their paradigms of success. In today's setting it is becoming more and more difficult to even understand the term 'core self'.

Working with your soul will cause you to think deeply not only about your own values and where they have come from, but about traditional collective values and those of the moment. Communication today is almost instant – you can know what is going on in far-flung places of the world even as it is happening. Not only do you know about it but you also receive instant visual images of it. Not so very long ago you might *never* have known about things that went on only a few miles away, let alone on the other side of the world. If you did hear about something it would often be when it was all over and resolved, and you could only participate retrospectively in grief, shock or celebration.

Clothes and your identity

Dreams, said by the Talmud to be 'messages from your soul', often contain sequences about being naked or exposed in some undignified situation. (For more about dreams see Chapter 9.) Such dream symbolism may be telling you how wary you are about coming into contact with, or letting it be seen, who or what you intrinsically are. Without clothes you are naked and vulnerable, there is no covering beneath which to hide, no style to help you project the image you either want to, or feel you should, project. Clothes give a changing identity and help you to fulfil different roles. Work clothes, interview clothes, party clothes, going-out clothes, relaxing-at-home clothes all help to express different parts of your multifaceted being.

Different clothes for different roles may also be linked to subpersonalities (see Chapter 6).

Conformity is not all bad, however. If your conformity is more or less confined to appropriate behaviour to each situation you embrace in life, and you have thought it through and are comfortable with it, a purpose may be served. Nevertheless, it is also possible to be in conformity overload and for it to hide the pathway to communication with your core self. Do you believe that how you dress is who you are? Do you dare to use dress as a way to express your individuality or do you feel compelled to follow trends and fashions?

Messengers of your true self

The things that cloud you from finding your core self and befog its light from shining forth are becoming more and more complex. When you are blocked from being able to express your true self because you are in any way afraid to fight for what you truly want or because you are overanxious about how others will react to the changes you want to make in your life, you can become subject to disease or 'the dark night of the soul'. In certain circumstances disease (or dis-ease) and the dark night are allies of the soul and of the core self, and have within them a wisdom of their own.

Nowadays, few talk about the dark night of the soul, even though a high proportion of people take some sort of medication for depression or stress. Illness and dark nights of the soul are related. Illness frequently *is* a dark night of the soul, not only for the sufferer but also for the loved and loving ones who try to offer support. Although not specifically highlighted in my telling of Sarah's story (page 122), it takes little imagination to realise that her brave recovery did not happen without the added challenge of the soul's dark night, not only for herself but also for those who loved and supported her.

Your soul is intent on helping you to find your core self, and your core self is also very powerful. If what society or others expect of you is way out of tune with the note of your true self, then, in various ways, you will eventually find yourself to be out of harmony. If you do not recognise this and make adjustments in your life, you may become ill, have an accident or go through a dark night of the soul. Illness often has its roots in the moment, where subconsciously your being recognises that you are out of touch with your core self. There are significant dangers attendant upon opting, either consciously or unconsciously, to live your life from the stance of your conditioned self. When your mind tries to shut down your emotions or core feelings, you can become entrenched in a commitment to goals that are the product of your conditioning and not of your intrinsic blueprint. When mind and emotions are in a power struggle, your body or your so-called 'sick self' may collude with your emotions. The body can become the servant of your emotions and your emotions are linked to the need of your core self to find sufficient expression. When your body fails, change may be forced upon you in order to awaken you.

Symbolic knocks on the head and kicks from behind

Sometimes your soul may employ symbolic knocks on the head and kicks from behind in order to challenge you with the need to implement change or to make you take serious stock of the status quo of your life. Accidents, which can also be full of symbolic meaning, may be caused by actual kicks from behind or knocks on the head whereas, symbolically, illness may be either of these.

Sarah did not get sick, but had a serious accident that most probably had powerful or contributory causes due to an implicit discrepancy between her core self and her conditioned self. She came through her suffering to find a fulfilment she believed she would not have found in her former lifestyle, exciting as it had been. In the midst of trauma, her core self emerged and gave her the strength to win through.

The collusion of emotions and body

When you learn to listen to your emotions and your body, and recognise the communication that exists between them, it is possible to understand the messages you are being given at as early a stage as possible. It can then be possible to choose change, actively and consciously, before the stage of kicks from behind and knocks on the head make change happen to you. Ideally you need to choose change before change chooses you.

It is more difficult to avoid the signals of your body than it is to continue to obey the structures of your conditioned mind. If your body is ill you cannot continue. If you ignore the messages of minor symptoms or a peripheral sense of unease or dis-ease, then you may actually develop a disease or ailment, have an accident or be plunged into a dark night of your soul. Of course, we all need to take an occasional remedy to relieve some minor bodily symptom, but if you find yourself doing it too regularly, or always on a certain day of the week, it is well worth looking to see whether there is a recurring pattern of reaction to certain things in your life. You might find that you are being urged through the collusion of emotions and body to look at how you might bring about the interaction and action that can create the changes that prevent the pattern from escalating.

Signals

Pain is a way of signalling when something is wrong, and not only at the purely physical level. The final tools of your emotions or the unheard pleas of your core self are to employ your body as a messenger. Your soul might also have an input here in that it may be endeavouring to signal frantically something of importance to you, its ambassador. If you merely kill pain with pills in order to carry on your lifestyle without interruptions, you might be missing an important message from your body and be in danger of leaving the real meaning and cause behind your trouble undetected. If you do not examine your life pattern, a serious illness or breakdown may develop. Recurring headaches can develop into heart attacks or strokes. Life-threatening illness forcing you to consider your quality of life can develop from symptoms you ignore or about which you go into denial. The consequences of a crisis in health often put our conditioned self under considerable scrutiny, or may even kill it off. This is the way in which disease can be an ally of the soul and the true self.

When you look carefully at your life after even a minor health crisis, it is possible to determine to make changes in attitude or circumstances that will foster a better quality of being for you. When you look at the symbolic price you may be paying in order to maintain certain values or lifestyle you may seriously wonder whether you might be in actual danger of killing yourself for standards that mean less than you previously thought or were conditioned to think. Being vigilant about your values and quality of life, and reassessing them on a regular basis, can help to modify your conditioned self so that you are able to keep optimum and finely balanced physical, mental, spiritual and emotional health.

Symptoms and their symbolism

Getting rid of symptoms is not enough. In order to decode the message that your body has been employed to convey to you, they have to be listened to, explored and thoroughly understood. Listening to symptoms at an early stage and treating them as symbols can mean that you do not need to become seriously ill in order to change the pattern or to get in touch with your core self. Symptoms can be seen as messages from your emotions and your core self that your body has been employed to deliver.

Part of working with your soul is to learn to think symbolically. Sensing the symbolism in symptoms of illness, or in the types of illness that you may be prone to, is therefore an important part of soul work. Your sick self can be a very wise self indeed, not only taking you away from untenable situations for a while but also, perhaps, opening a special door to self-knowledge that will first of all invite you, but perhaps eventually oblige you, to make a life change that you eventually recognise as being life-enhancing.

Sometimes the way in which we speak of symptoms can give us a very clear clue as to their symbolism or origin:

'My job gives me a pain in the neck.'

'I can't stomach the amount of work I have to do.'

'I need a break.' (On a personal note beware of this one! I realise that I was saying it to myself without taking action on it and spent a long time recovering from a broken ankle that gave me an enforced break in many ways!)

'There is too much weight on my shoulders.'

'It makes my stomach churn,'

... and the many more such common phrases.

Getting better

When Gildas, my discarnate guide, speaks of illness and disease, he advises you to define or redefine exactly what you mean when you seek to 'get better' or well again. All too often you probably mean that you want to get back to a state of health you have previously known in order to continue life as you have previously known it. He suggests that illness invites you to move on into a state of health that you have never previously known. It is a cata-lyst for you to be able to do that, by taking a review of your life, understanding the symbolism of your symptoms and by making both attitudinal and circumstantial change in order to find the lifestyle, work or way of being that releases and maximises the potential of your core self. To do this you need at least some understanding of the symbolism of disease.

The symbolism of disease

Every symptom carries a different message. Although there may be a common thread in the message carried by a particular group of symptoms, the total communication to the individual manifesting such symptoms is unique and personal. Lists suggesting categorical meanings for symptoms should be used only as a guide to further personal insight. To be told that trouble with a gall bladder means that you are unconsciously bitter may have some truth in it because of the symbolism of bitter gall. However, such categorical definition includes all gall bladders that give trouble and every person that has gall-bladder trouble. It does not take any account of personal circumstances or personal association to the symbol of a troubled gall bladder.

Is *your* gall bladder producing stones? Too much or too little gall? Which foods does it react to? There are so many subsidiary questions you might ask before being certain about what *your* gall-bladder symptoms mean. Categorical information about symptoms might also err towards making you feel over-responsible. To be told that you are bitter might evoke guilt or shame. To be asked to consider what bitter pill life has dealt you that has been difficult to swallow is a very different approach.

Illness today

There are still many things that current medical practice cannot heal. It may be clever at bringing symptomatic relief, although all too often this can be achieved only by causing others or with side effects. When symptoms are relieved, you expect, and are expected, to get back to work or the daily routines as soon as possible. Illness in our times has become an industry employing and giving livelihood to millions of people and giving rise to many connected industries. If everyone who is ill today were to get better tomorrow, the world economy would probably not survive. There is therefore an implicit message, or hidden agenda, that a certain proportion of people need to remain sick. The explicit message of our society, however, is: be well, be healthy, get over your illness as soon as possible, mask your symptoms, take pills that bring you out of depression or give you distance from its causes. In many cases this leads to an unconscious pretence that it is *not* really happening and can lead to despair of all kinds. The messages around us are very mixed indeed.

Dark nights of the soul

Thomas Moore, who wrote the book *Dark Nights of the Soul* said, 'the chief malady in our time is sleeping soul sickness'. Society in general praises and encourages the conditioned well self while investing heavily in illness. Those who are engaged in spiritual or religious pursuits spend a lot of time praising the light and often do not know how to help those who are out of touch with their souls or who feel that their souls may be asleep or have abandoned them. There is also not enough help around if you happen to be asleep to the purposes of your soul.

If your soul seems to be asleep to you or you have gone to sleep on soul matters, then although they are rarely now spoken of as such, you may well be experiencing a dark night of the soul. Too often the dark night is no longer seen as a time when spiritual counsel may be needed, but is given the label of depression and passed over to the medical doctor rather than to the priest or the spiritual consultant. Even in religious and spiritual circles the phrase 'curing of souls' is now rarely heard. On the other hand, if you are open to the different ways of spiritual intervention and are experiencing a dark night of the soul, shamans, discarnate guides, healers and transpersonal therapists can be consulted.

The fear of darkness

The danger with the dark night of the soul, as also with depression, can be that even such effective interventionists as shamans and others who take the dimension of soul into account in their work, may want to bring you out of the dark journey too urgently. There is an almost universal fear of darkness. All who see a loved one going into a dark journey will, of course, want to bring them back as soon as possible, but we need to question whether this actually *is* the best approach. Bringing back or seeking to lift someone out of a depression or dark night of the soul implies that there is no intrinsic pattern in the experience and that the quicker you can be lifted from the dark into the light, the better will it be.

Of course, if you are in a depression or a dark night of the soul you need to know that there is a way out. You also need to know that the experience has a purpose. In depression it feels as if all momentum has been lost, but though the pace may be slow, it can still be seen as a journey. To say that there is light at the end of the tunnel can seem trite and is not necessarily helpful to someone in darkness, if it is said with the wrong timing. Depression is a lonely experience and for those who see it as a dark night of the soul's abandonment it can be even more intensively so. Sometimes all that can be done at a certain stage is to try to reassure the one who travels through such a dark night that even if they cannot feel it they are being accompanied (see Evelyn's story, page 145). Even if they cannot see it, to know that a friend is staying near and in touch, and holding a steady light on their behalf, can give hope that they will eventually also be able to see its glow.

Climbing upwards into the light

Many who draw or paint the dark journey show it as a journey down into dark earth or water where at one point the downward movement levels out and an upward journey gradually begins. The climb upwards is by no means vertical but curves steadily to the surface once more. The point of exit from the darkness is never the same point as that of the entry. It is a new place, with a different view or perspective. If, when in a dark journey you are exhorted to come out too soon, ignoring the natural rhythm or cycle of the journey, there is a danger of returning to the same point at which you entered the darkness, like being hauled up from a hole into which you have fallen. No true journey from outset to destination will have been made, no inner resolution will have been found, no different vista is there on emergence, and the dilemma or despair may be prone to re-occur too readily. The night will not have passed in its own way to its own moment of light or dawn. It is possible to be pulled or forced out into the fast-fading light of a false day.

The womb that enables the wonderful process of gestation of new life is dark. We all know that you cannot pull a growing foetus out of that dark place until its gestation is accomplished and its due moment of birth has arrived. The dark night of the soul can be about the death of your conditioned self followed by the gestation, discovery and birth of your core self.

Neither depression nor a dark night of the soul is a pleasant experience, but if it is seen as a journey that can be accompanied, then, like any night, it will often work its way through the dark hours or dark cycles to the light in its own time. If you are travelling through such an experience, it is important to come through to the point of the new dawn or the new day and not to come back to the same point as the one at which the experience began. Similar to illness, there is, beyond the depths, the potential for a state of health that has never before been known or experienced. As a society we have lost touch with natural cycles and rhythms and do not find it easy to 'trust the process' or the innate wisdom carried in each one of us.

Having said all this, I am of course aware that biochemistry can play a part in depression and the darker journeys of life known to us. I am not an advocate of always assuming that nature will take its course and I am aware of the dangers that accompany deep depression, but having seen that both illness and depression can lead to a fuller recognition of the core self, then I make my plea for such happenings to at least be looked at as having potential in the business of working with your soul.

Does your soul abandon you?

So, in a dark night of the soul, where is your soul? Dante, in his *Inferno* described the dark night of the soul as follows:

'In the middle of our life journey I found myself in a dark wood. I had wandered from the straight path. It isn't easy to talk about it:

it was such a thick, wild, and rough forest that when I think of it my fear returns ... I can't offer any good explanation for how I entered it. I was so sleepy at that point that I strayed from the right path.'

Conditioning puts you to sleep in terms of being able to follow the path of your core self. In sleep you dream. In a dark night of the soul, strange and perhaps frightening dreams are often a part of the experience. If dreams are messages from your soul and if a dark night leads to the new dawn, the most likely place for your soul to be is right there beside you, accompanying you through the darkness until you fully awaken once more at the due time, to realise that things have to change and that you can be the arbiter of that change. Conditioning not only puts you to sleep, it dulls your senses so that you lose awareness that your soul and all your angels, guides and helpers are watching over you, not from far away, but from nearby, so as to greet you at the very moment that your awakening to the new dawn or the birth of your true self begins to alight within you. Conditioning makes you blind to the presence of your soul and to any sense of purpose or continuity, but your soul keeps you in sight at all times. (There is more about dreams and the presence of guides, helpers and angels in the following chapter.)

Chronic illness and disability as soul service

If part of working with your soul is about learning to think symbolically, then it is also necessary to learn to think symbolically about society and the collective in order to put your own personal symbols and aspects of working with your soul and your soul service into a wider context (see also Chapter 6).

There is a common tendency or temptation to see the difficulties of life as karmic punishment resulting from causes set in motion in previous lifetimes. Many people, therefore, especially those who endure chronic sickness or disability, may believe that *this* is a form of karmic punishment. This also applies to those who are born with incurable conditions or handicaps. I have known instances where others have actually speculated about what past sins have been committed that are now being punished in this way. This train of thought is, to my mind, very limited and mistaken. It can be particularly difficult when also applied to those who give birth to children who are not seen to be 'normal'.

The view that Gildas teaches is that chronic disease, disability and inborn conditions can certainly be part of the soul's choice or contract, *sometimes* for reasons of retributive karma, although certainly not for reasons of punishment. Retributive karma is linked to retributive soul work. He sees several reasons why this might be so and also that many incarnating personality beads, who in consultation with their souls have chosen such difficulties, are beads from soul stems that may be nearing the end of their incarnate experience or evolution.

Since the soul seeks all experiences that can be a possible part of incarnation on earth, it follows that it may, at some time in its evolutionary journey, choose to give one of its incarnating beads the experience of lifetime illness or disability. This tendency of the soul to sometimes choose very difficult incarnations may, at first sight seem callous, but wholeness of knowledge and experience has to be all inclusive, not just selective of that which is easy, beautiful or harmonious. Soul work includes a certain amount of suffering, but also the opportunity to bring something special out of that suffering. Thus, according to the strength of the soul to give the necessary support, there come those moments in its evolution where a bead incarnates with a heavy burden to carry.

The effects of illness on others

When the burden is one of illness or disability, many others will also be affected. We are, inevitably, catalysts for each other. Parents, relatives, carers, doctors, nurses, teachers are all involved in the lives of those who need considerable support just to live through each day and, above all, to be able to enjoy any quality of life. There are many who are thus involved who speak of how much they learn from both the courage and the suffering of others. It can be a humbling experience. Those who need such care are often teachers of toler-ance, compassion, appreciation of the more basic values of life and much more. They inspire others to fund-raise, start organisations, charities and support groups, and in their need may be instrumen-tal in creating empathetic bonds among those whose lives would not have been given the same kind of depth without these shared chal-lenges. A great deal of selfless and unconditional love is often generated that cannot help but touch into the collective human experience.

It can be seen then, that as well as choosing a physically difficult life as part of the full spectrum of incarnate experience, the soul may also give the bead who undertakes that experience an agenda or contract for teaching others compassion, unconditional love, re-thinking of life values, dedication and service. They also, of course, may be inspirers of creative invention and medical research.

Personal and collective evolution

Evolution is collective as well as individual. The whole of humanity is evolving and the contribution of every incarnate soul bead resonates with that evolution and furthers the total human journey. A proportion of humanity is sick or ill at any given time. As an indi-vidual you may have to experience illness as part of the catalyst that enables you to make contact with your true or core self. The pathway to positive health on every level usually involves change. You might recover from one illness and return to your old patterns and think that you are 'better' again. But unless the wisdom, symbolism and intrinsic message from your soul that is held within the disease has been read and understood it may well not be long before you are ill again. Recurring illness is a message from your soul asking you to look at what needs to change in your life. When you stop and take stock you embrace the opportunity to be healed in the truest sense so that you move on to that state of positive health that you have never known before.

In collective terms if those individuals who are ill seek the messages and wisdom that lie in the depths of disease, so they contribute their own healing to the healing of the collective body of humankind, thus making it possible that eventually the whole of humanity may find and function from its collective core self. When this happens, we shall, so most discarnate guides tell us, have entered into a new and golden age where the true potential of humanity can blossom fragrantly and fully. To be a part of this is soul work, or even soul service. Your soul contract may include a commitment to enabling change at a wider level. Part of the contract, then, to incarnate to a life of illness or disability might be to act as one of a group serving a particular cause to further the collective understanding and attainment of health.

Similarly, part of your soul contract may include other work for the collective, such as helping to find the creative balance between the collective masculine and feminine principles. In our present times there is a great deal of activity in the field of understanding male and female roles so that each can be valued for its intrinsic nature and brought into the right relationship with the other. This is also a process of healing a collective dis-ease that contributes to the attainment of a golden age, not only for humankind but also for the universe. At some point or for some purpose in the wide meanings that healing can have, we all have issues related to collective evolution included in our soul contracts.

Being true to your core self

A major part of working with your soul is to learn to be true to your core self. Illness and dark nights of the soul force us to take note. I am sure that our souls have no investment in causing or wishing us to be ill or to go through personal and inner dark nights when we feel abandoned and lost. Illness and dark soul nights come from within ourselves at times when it may be imperative for us to awaken from the sleep and illusion of conditioning into a knowledge of our creative ability to shape our own lives as an art form and to know this as true soul work.

Although illness and dark nights of the soul should not be courted, in the transpersonal field it is often said that breakdown may be necessary to break through. At such times we may become conscious of our ability to remove barriers we had not realised were imprisoning us, cross thresholds we hardly knew were there and learn to embrace life in a far more meaningful and fulfilling way. It is then, also, that we may awaken to a sense of the way in which we are working with our souls and our souls are working with us to high purpose.

Sarah's story illustrates some of the points I have made in this chapter about accident, illness and the unexpected. Evelyn's story is of someone going through a dark night of the soul, knowing that even though she is not being able truly to feel that she was being accompanied through her dark time, she eventually comes out on the other side of it to a new joy and purpose in life.

Evelyn's story

A sudden and tragic shock brought on Evelyn's dark night of the soul. She and her husband, Simon, had been together for many years. They ran a successful business organising exhibitions of various kinds. They personified most people's idea of a 'golden couple' with their many shared interests, wide circle of friends, and ability to enjoy life to the full. They had no obvious health problems. It was totally unexpected and particularly tragic, then, when Simon, having for once gone on ahead of Evelyn to organise the early stages of an exhibition, was found dead of a heart attack in his hotel bed.

Everyone who knew Evelyn and Simon were totally shocked. Evelyn, as might be expected, was devastated, the more so because of it being so very unexpected and because Simon had died alone. She took care of all the practical arrangements with great courage and fortitude, but it soon became obvious that despite all the support and concern of friends she was not coping well.

Her son from a previous marriage lived in America and he and his wife arranged to come to England on an extended stay to support his mother and to try to help her to manage her grief and take up some quality of life again. He encouraged Evelyn to make one of her trusted colleagues a full business partner so that the work she had always loved could continue. For over a year Evelyn's son worked alongside her and her trusted colleague helping to keep the thriving business going. Evelyn said that this was what she wanted most, in Simon's memory and out of respect for him. She wanted to take an increasing part in the work and resume her former role. In fact, however, she sank deeper and deeper into depression, shut herself away more and more and was unable to enjoy the extended visit of her son, daughter-in-law and grandchildren.

She began to take long retreats in a convent where she was well looked after and sympathetically received. Although not religious in a conventional way, Evelyn had always practised meditation. Now she said she received comfort from the ordered simplicity and peace that was available to her as a guest at the convent. She drew support from the services she was allowed to attend and from the sung music.

It seemed that Evelyn was reaching a new stage in her mourning and beginning to recover from her severe shock and stress. She confided to her son that she was also seeking spiritual meaning for the collapse of all that she had held dear. She began to be more visible and competent again in her company role, although she still took every sixth week off to go to the convent.

Her son began to make plans to return to America where he had a full life of his own. His children were longing to return to their normal life, their familiar schools and their friends. It was another big and completely unexpected shock then, for all concerned, when, on Evelyn's next visit to the convent, she was found in the nick of time, having taken an overdose of antidepressants that secretly and determinedly she had been storing up over a period of time.

She was resuscitated in hospital and referred for psychiatric help. Before Evelyn met Simon, she had attended some of my workshops. She now got in touch, and asked if I would visit her in the psychiatric unit to which she had been admitted after two more overdose incidents. When I went to see her she said that she had lost any sense of meaning in life and no longer believed in any higher power or higher purpose.

She insisted that she would definitely take every possible opportunity to end her own life. I asked her if this was because she felt that death would bring her to a reunion with Simon. She replied that she had no faith in any afterlife any more and now believed that death was actually nothing more than 'ashes to ashes and dust to dust'. This was what she longed for, to be annihilated, without consciousness or feeling.

Evelyn had reached rock bottom. She said that if there was by any chance a Higher Being, which she totally doubted, she was too angry with the havoc that life could become to want to relate to anything of that kind. She had always thought that she had strong inner resources but now felt she had none. She felt abandoned by God, or that maybe God was dead or had never been. She could only see life as an unending dark tunnel.

She was very unhappy in hospital and felt further abandoned by her son. It had become urgent and imperative for him to return to America very soon. Evelyn refused all invitations for her to go back with him, where he promised to keep an eye on her and to seek all the best treatments and support for her. All that I felt able to do for her was to assure her that her terrible dark tunnel could still lead to the light and have a very different end than her physical death. Together with others I reminded her that there were many people alongside her who believed that her life *could* take off for her once more and that we would continue to hold that faith even though she could not, at that time, hold it for herself. We told her that we *knew* that she had those deep inner resources that she presently felt she had never had.

It took time, but gradually, constantly reminded that even though her darkness might be so great that she could not see or feel us, and that we were not going to go away or stop holding the light of hope for her, Evelyn began to listen to some of the music she had always loved. She asked for the books that contained the poetry she had always read, and from which she had drawn delight, inspiration and spiritual sustenance. We gradually noticed that she was also listening to the kind of music that she and Simon had enjoyed together. She now occasionally spoke of him without the anger that she had previously felt because he had seemingly abandoned her without warning. 'He left me without even saying goodbye', was a sentence she had often repeated both piteously and with bitter anger and resentment.

She told her doctors that she was ready for her medication to be reduced. She felt as though her 'head was beginning to clear'. Some of her own spirit returned and she began to discuss how we felt that Simon would have wanted her to handle this extreme crisis. Perhaps one of the moments of greatest breakthrough for her was when she wrote and shared with her close friends a poem about the abandonment felt in her dark night of the soul but the spark of hope that was gradually igniting in her heart, that there *was* a light at the end of the tunnel and that there was meaningful work for her to do.

Most of us felt that Simon would have wanted Evelyn to handle the crisis by carrying their business on and forward, but Evelyn felt that if Simon had lived they would eventually have conceived another venture. 'We had accumulated a wealth of financial resources and investments,' she said, 'as well as a great deal of expertise in "showcasing". Before Simon died, we had begun to talk to each other about how we could perhaps use some of our resources and expertise less selfishly and look at ways in which we might leave our mark in the world by "making a difference"'. She told us that at moments when her darkest darkness had begun to lift and bring her hope of a dawn, she had touched into a feeling that when it came she should use what she called 'this new day of my life' in a very different way.

It did not happen all at once, or without setbacks, but Evelyn eventually found her niche in a voluntary organisation working to raise funds for a number of very worthy causes. She became a generous donor to this organisation but also found with them a welcome for the adaptable skills of her business acumen and was invited to join their fund-raising team. She accepted this opportunity and was successful in helping them to raise their profile considerably.

One of the most memorable things she said to me was: 'My soul and Simon's soul are blessing this work. The dark night I went through was deep and terrible and at one time I was determined not to emerge from it. I know though, that without it, this particular dawn would never have come. I know that I have found my true self, and although on one level I shall always be lonely without Simon, on another I am deeply fulfilled and can await our reunion not only with patience but with joy in the interim.'

Exercise on finding the seed of your true self

The exercise for this chapter is one of meditative reflection and drawing to help you to find an image for the seed of your true self. You will also find another image for the flowering, fruiting or blossoming that the seed of your true self can produce, when properly recognised and nurtured. It is based on the process that Plato referred to as 'entelechy': the seed, or blueprint, can only, but gloriously, become what it has within it the potential to become. Before you begin, read through Preparing for the Exercises on page 5.

Exercise 10: entelechy – the seed and the becoming

Have your special notebook or sheets of paper and crayons, pastels or paints to hand. For this reflection you might like to use crayons or paint to help your imagery while you are actually in reflective mode, but you can also use them later, when your initial reflections come to an end.

1. Make sure that you will be comfortable and undisturbed. Find your comfortable position.

2. Focus on the rhythm of your breathing. Be aware of each

in-breath and out-breath, do not try to alter your breath rhythm in any particular way, but allow it to find its natural level and flow.

3. Sense your breath as coming in and out at the 'petals' of your heart centre or chakra (life energy centre). This lies in the centre of your body and aura on the same level as your physical heart (see Glossary).

4. As your regular breathing helps your heart chakra to open, get a sense of entering your own inner space or dimension.

5. You are seeking an image for the blueprint of your true self. The obvious image would be of some kind of seed, and this may be right for you, but at first, resist it, and see if any more unusual or less familiar image comes to you. If the image of a seed persists, endeavour to examine it innerly, very carefully and see what form it has, what colours it may embody and what environment may be around it.

6. As the image forms, take your special notebook or a sheet of paper and your colours or paints and draw the image meditatively. As you draw in this way the image may develop. Allow yourself free licence for this to happen.

7. Contemplate what you have seen within and what you have drawn for about 5 minutes, endeavouring to absorb how this feels as well as how it looks.

8. Put the paper or book page on which you have drawn your image of your blueprint or seed to one side.

9. Return to your heart breath.

10. Imagine that your blueprint is growing and becoming – gradually releasing the potential that it holds.

11. You may be aware of definite stages of growth, as from seed to root, to shoot, to leaf, to bud, to flower and to fruit. If these images are at first linked to images of a plant growing, stay alongside them, but see also if different or more unusual images develop.

12. Take paper and crayons or paints, or a page in your special notebook and draw the images that are coming into your awareness. As you draw intuitively the images may develop in their own way, or backgrounds may be added. Give yourself free licence for this to happen as you draw from your heart.

13. Spend some time contemplating all the images you have drawn or your blueprint and your becoming for up to 15 minutes.

14. Ask yourself whether there is a question that you would like to ask about what you have drawn or about the inner process you have been through in pursuing this exercise.

15. If a question presents itself, write it down either in outline or as fully as possible.

16. When you are ready, become conscious of the whole of your body and where you are sitting in your normal, every-day world.

17. Feel your contact with the ground, open your eyes and connect with your outer surroundings, before closing them again in order to visualise a cloak of light, with a hood, right around you.

The full or outline question that you may have written will be used in Exercise 11 at the end of the next chapter so, as you move on through that chapter, keep your question in mind or go on endeavouring to form it.

Chapter 9 looks at the role of the guidance of dreams, discarnate guides and angelic beings in working with your soul.

9

Listening to Your Soul

The purposes of your soul for your present incarnation, its contract with you, and its desire for you to be its ambassador for continued evolution give your life shape. If you are ready to work more consciously with your soul, then part of your task is to discern the shape your life is taking and to use that shape to help you to recognise that the ultimate in working with your soul is to find your true, or core self.

How your soul communicates with you

Your soul may often seem diffuse and distant. Direct communication with it is not easy, although can, with practice, be achieved. Exercise 1 on page 7 and Exercise 8 on page 99 aim to help in this process. Endeavouring to decode your soul contract may seem like trying to pick up a trail that is difficult to follow. Life, frustratingly, may seem to be made up of a series of crossroads with no clear signposts. If you go through a dark night of the soul you can feel that your soul has withdrawn from you or allowed you to go to sleep. Yet *at all times*, if you truly look, your soul *is* endeavouring to communicate with you, not only by the givens and challenges in your life and by relying on you to decode these, but through your dreams, your discarnate guides and helpers, and through the guardianship of the angelic realms.

Although in our present times there is great interest in discarnate guidance as well as the subtle realms and presence of angels, for some people these particular aspects may seem to be esoteric in the extreme. You may feel extremely tentative towards them. Of all the subtle areas of experience, dreams are at least a commonly shared encounter with areas beyond the mundane, although they are often regarded as extraordinary.

Dreams as communication from your soul

You may be fascinated by your dreams and the apparent enigmas their imagery presents. You may or may not be interested in keeping records of them and in learning to understand the wonderful messages they often give. You may see them as a phenomenon of life but not value them as part of the working of your soul to communicate with you. You may say, 'I never dream', or, 'I only dream after I have eaten cheese or drunk too much wine.' You may fear your dreams, or dismiss them because they seem too complex or strange. You may say that you dream only rarely, or not at all. It has, however, been scientifically proven that we all dream and that when deprived of dreaming sleep our mental and physical health can suffer. If you think you are a non-dreamer, what you actually mean is that you do not remember your dreams.

The importance of dreams

The Talmud famously says that 'Dreams are letters from your Soul'. This puts them on a sacred level, suggesting that if you want to work more consciously with your soul it behoves you to learn to acknowledge them and perhaps to be able to read their symbolism in depth. Psychologists such as Sigmund Freud and C.G. Jung placed great importance on the need to understand your dreams as a means to a deeper understanding of yourself. Ancient and some so-called primitive cultures greatly valued dreams and the dreamers of dreams. The ancient Egyptians and Greeks used dream interpretation as an aid to healing maladies of soul, spirit, body and mind.

Scientists believe that while you dream your brain is sifting through your reactions to life and its events in order to sort and store them. It can be difficult to admit some reactions and responses to life into fully conscious awareness and this is why dreams have a symbolic code of their own. There are things that your inner censor discards or pushes deep down into your psyche. The sometimes seemingly obscure symbolism within dreams occurs because of this censoring process. To get at, and admit into full awareness, these deep inner observations, requires self-work and openness. This can be richly rewarding in expanding self-knowledge and spiritual growth and in learning to hear what your soul is endeavouring to say to you, that you might also in some way be shutting out or reluctant to face.

As dreams hold such important communications, both from within your psyche and from dimensions beyond, it is well worth the effort required to improve your dream recall and to learn to understand and appreciate more fully the potentially rich world your dreams can access.

When you become more at home in the territory of dreams, you open up a potential for your soul to use your dreaming time as a means of showing you a way forward or of sending you messages that otherwise your more conscious mental processes might block.

The power and wonder of symbols has already been mentioned in Chapter 6. Dreams are a very fertile ground for bringing you the kind of symbols that it is important to observe, listen to and work with. This is not the place to write a full guide to dream recall and interpretation but some simple measures often suffice to make you more conversant with the richness of your dream life and language. If you want to make a fuller study there are books for further reading, recommended in the Bibliography.

Remembering your dreams

If the first stage for you is learning to *remember* your dreams, have a notebook and pen beside your bed and as soon as you wake write down your first thoughts. Make a note of the feeling quality you sense, as you wake. If there is some vaguely remembered snippet of a dream, do not dismiss it, but write it down. Doing this will signal to your psyche that you want to listen to, and partake in, the dialogue of your dreams. Gradually your dream recall should increase. A more drastic measure is to set an alarm clock to wake you after every one-and-a-half hours of sleep. Scientific study of dreams has concluded that we enter dreaming sleep about every one and a half hours during the night. If you wake yourself up when you are still close to a phase of dreaming sleep, you are more likely to remember what you were dreaming about.

At first, don't try to understand or interpret your dreams, unless you are used to doing so. Simply notice whatever you can, note it down and from time to time re-read and reflect on what you have written and what you have learned from, and about, your dream life. You may notice that dreams have similar themes, and if you use a loose-leaf notebook to record your dreams or dream snippets, you can arrange them according to these themes. For example, my own dream journal contains several dreams that have a Victorian setting and a similar feeling to them, there is a section of marriage dreams, one about horses, another about the sea, ships and dolphins and a large section about houses.

Finding the messages

The more you write things down and simply reflect on what you have written, the more will you begin to get a sense of the messages held within your dreams. Sometimes sharing such a process with a friend or partner will help to open up the dream language, even before you endeavour to learn more about the very special way in which dreams use symbols.

Dreams are clever. Everything in them has meaning. One way of looking at them is to see every part of your dream as a part of yourself. In this way you never assume that if you dream about a friend, partner or relative, the dream is telling you something about that individual. The dream's messages are for you, and so it is important to reflect upon what that person means for you, or in you. The question to ask is: what does this person teach me about myself?

Numbers may refer to certain years in your life, or take you back to different ages. They may refer to a number of days, weeks or months previously, as well as to years. Words in dreams may also be puns or contain word play. A client dreamed a dream about her current values. One of the symbols in the dream was a cashmere coat – an outer covering that is often highly prized – but as she worked on the dream she realised that the word 'cashmere' was also 'mere cash'. This discovery meant a great deal to her in her life at that time and in her dream-interpretation process.

Symbolism

Because most things in dreams are symbolic, dreams that contain death or birth do not necessarily mean that an actual death or birth is about to occur. A dream about death may be telling you, quite positively, that something in your life needs to be left behind or allowed to 'die' symbolically. Birth dreams may tell you that you can give birth to a whole new phase in your life or to something creative and new.

It is possible for you to have precognitive dreams in which you see something happening and then later it takes place, just as you had dreamed. This is a comparatively rare phenomenon but if you have had such a dream, it is all too easy to assume that most of your dreams will in some way, be precognitive. This may not be an entirely comfortable feeling to live with. I would therefore advise you to consult a counsellor who is experienced in dream work to help to put such dreams into proportion and enable you to become more comfortable with your dreaming self and the riches it can reveal.

Incubating a dream

Once you become interested in your dreams, you will realise how fertile they can be in giving you self-knowledge and higher perspective. It is then worth endeavouring to 'incubate' a dream for guidance when you have a perplexing issue to explore. The rule of three applies. I usually light a candle three nights running, just before I go to bed. As I light the candle, I focus on the issue I want to explore more deeply and ask my dreaming self, in conjunction with my soul, to give me a dream about it. I then sit quietly with the candle for another two or three minutes and blow it out, asking my dreaming self, or the part of me that forms my dreams, to send me an appropriate or insightful dream. Sometimes the dream comes immediately on the first night, sometimes it does not come even on the third night, but I light the candle only three times for this purpose. The dream rarely fails to come, even if it is two or three weeks later. 'Nagging' at the dreaming self does not work. It will respond in its own time and in its own way.

Dreams and dark nights of the soul

Vivid, and what might appear to be terrible dreams, are sometimes part of the process known as 'the dark night of the soul', as discussed in Chapter 8. It is a time when it is possible to have those dark and intense dreams often referred to as nightmares. I firmly believe that all dreams have, within them, a positive message, no matter how terrible and upsetting the actual dreaming scenario might seem to be. The nightmare might be described as the dark side of the dream, but often, if it is challenged, its insistent pattern will stop, and most nightmares can be worked with in such a way as to find the positive scenario beyond the fear and disturbance.

A dark night dream
A dreamer, going through a dark night of the soul, dreamed a repetitive dream:

'I am a rotting corpse in a deep and forsaken hole in the earth. My flesh is being eaten away by worms, beetles, birds and even rats and foxes. I know that soon the rats and foxes will start to gnaw at and devour my bones. Although I am a rotting corpse, I am aware that my dreaming self is dreaming this dream as a message for me and that the corpse is only a part of myself, but I am terrified and nauseated by the smell of rotting flesh that is very present at every moment of my dream. I dream the dream almost every night. I wake up from it trembling and sweating. I am haunted by it throughout every day. I feel there is no escape.'

The therapist for this woman suggested that in the safety of the therapy room and with the therapist alongside, the dream should be revisited in an attempt to understand more about it. It took great courage for this to happen. The woman entered an altered state of consciousness, only slightly different from full waking awareness, and went into active imagination, bravely re-entering her dream. As she looked tremulously at the rotting corpse she saw that a bird that came to feed from it needed food in order to be strong enough to carry out the exhausting routine of nurturing its nest of young. It had left some feathers in the cavities of the corpse. Worms had left worm casts; beetles, foxes and rats had left their dung.

As she looked into the symbolism of these things she saw that the feathers were a hope that she would eventually fly again, the worm casts and dung, and even the rotting flesh on the corpse, were compost breaking down old patterns but also capable of nurturing new growth. She began to accept this somewhat grisly dream as a gift from her dreaming self and her soul helping her to recognise that what was dead and rotten was what needed to be allowed to be so. The feathers were indeed a symbol of life and new flight. She knew that she needed compost for the growth of the plant of her core self. Just before she came out of the active imagination, she had a vision of light on water, which for her was a symbol of rebirth. She realised that the dawn was coming and that although there was still much to be released and worked upon, her dark night was nearing its end.

It took some time for these realisations to be worked out in the full arena of her everyday life but her dawn came in its own rhythm and timing. She made considerable changes in her life, saw clearly how to fly free from old and imprisoning conditioning and joyfully discovered the integrity of her core self.

Spirit guides

I have referred frequently to my own spirit, or discarnate guide, Gildas. I have drawn on his teachings as a basis for the framework of reference upon which the concept of working with your soul, given here, is set.

As a channel for Gildas, when I move into a slightly altered state of consciousness, I am aware of a communication with him. This takes the form of 'hearing' or knowing words that he drops into my mind like a kind of dictation. I have been aware of a discarnate being accompanying me since I was about three years old, and when I was 18 and training to be a teacher I channelled Gildas formally for the first time. I have now been working with him for 50 years.

Guides are part of the organisation of your soul. Usually they are evolved beads from your soul thread who have moved on to be distinct entities in a somewhat different form of life, where they oversee, offer guardianship, teach and heal. If not from your personal soul thread then they may be from your soul group (see Chapter 2). You all have discarnate helpers, and at least one guide, to help your souls to watch over you. These beings guide you, guard you, and make sure that as an ambassador for your soul you are in the right place at the right time. They support your choices, as well as making you aware of alternatives, so that you realise that you *have* choices and the power to implement them.

How guides might communicate

Not all guides communicate as directly or in the same way as Gildas. They will however, help to organise meaningful synchronicities in your life, make sure you meet the right person at the right time, read the right book at the right time, hear the right radio programme or see something on television that moves you and gives you a different or new perspective. They will be doing this whether you are aware of it or not, but as soon as you start actively to ask for guidance, you will find that such happenings in your life tend to increase.

Some of you who have not already done so, may be interested in taking the journey to be able to communicate more fully with your guide. Others of you may be content with the indirect type of communication mentioned in the previous paragraph. Obviously, although they are complementary areas, learning to work with your guide can be as complex a process as learning to work with your soul. Issues of guidance are fully explored in my book *Working With Spirit Guides* (see Bibliography).

Angels

Guides are part of the human stream of consciousness and are therefore different from angels. At a different level, guides are part of your soul thread and will have lived out many incarnations on earth. Guides and humans will never be angels and angels will never be incarnate. This is because angels belong to a different consciousness stream than the human. They form a collective body, within which there is mutual support and an evolutionary pattern.

Angels emanate from the Divine Source and are divided into groups, each of which has a specific task or area of interest. The main esoteric teachings about angels come from Zoroastrian and Hebraic sources, but belief in angels is woven into the fabric of humanity's spiritual search. From untutored reverence through to myths, tribal belief systems and every form of religious practice, angels have consistently been recipients of prayer as well as invited guests at celebrations and rituals.

Angels bring light and laughter into your life as well as helping you to arrive at a wider understanding of divinity, infinity and the scheme of the universe. They are certainly employed by your soul to help you find that path through life that maintains a full connection with the purposes of your soul and to help to prevent you from being in the wrong place at the wrong time.

The angelic hierarchy

There is a traditional angelic hierarchy in which there are three main angelic spheres. (There are books in the Bibliography where you can read up on these if you wish to do so.) The level at which your soul uses angels to watch over you and to help in bringing you its messages is much more informal and I shall proceed to explain more about that.

In the 'lower ranks' of the traditional angelic hierarchy are 'Angels without other titles' including your personal guardian angel. Others are named according to angelic qualities, such as light, love, healing, peace, faith, trust, delight, joy, humour, and many more. The angelic realms are vast realms of light. The angelic beings are diffuse and infinite until you have need of them. When you call for specific angelic help, it is as though a part of that diffuse and infinite angel consciousness detaches itself from a vast pool of light and subtle being, and comes in answer to your call, bringing the angelic quality you have named or asked for.

Angels' appearance

There are, on the market, numerous sets of angel cards. The first of these were designed at Findhorn, a long-standing spiritual community in Scotland (see Glossary). With this type of pack you can intuitively draw an angel to bless the day or night for you. You can draw one when you are in a quandary and need some spiritual help and support or inspiration. These cards have become popular because they have a lightness about them that perhaps reminds us that 'angels can fly because they take themselves lightly' (G.K. Chesterton).

Angels have traditional representation in art, where they are often portrayed as full of light and colour, shimmering and with wings.

Where something subtle has acquired a certain traditional representation it can often mean that the consensus of opinion represents that which those who are sensitive enough actually see. Angels are radiant energetic beings or shafts of light who move at a high level of vibration. It is the shimmering and the high vibrational level that give them the appearance of having wings. It is unlikely that they have actual bodies or countenances, but when they want to reveal themselves to you, they temporarily take on a form that you will recognise, or they surround you with a felt presence of something very light and tender.

A high proportion of people, who may not be particularly active in their spiritual life and beliefs, when asked categorically if they have seen an angel or felt an angelic presence will answer in the affirmative.

Guardian angels

Gildas teaches that your guardian angel comes into being at the moment your soul conceives the idea that you, a personality bead from its thread, will come into incarnation. This angelic being then watches over you through your conception, gestation and birth, is with you for the whole of your life, watches over your dying process and does not move on until you are well settled in the afterlife.

Part of the guardianship your personal guardian angel gives you is to ensure that you do not die before your life has followed its natural cycle, whether that is long or short. Your angel cannot protect you from difficult experiences, but it subtly helps you through and often stops the worst from happening. It works in close liaison with your soul and the implementation of your soul contract, especially in regard to finding your true self. The more you become angelically aware, the more you will begin to recognise the companionship and presence of your guardian angel, especially when you face difficult times or have important decisions to make.

If you look more closely at life and become more and more involved in your desire to understand its plan and yourself in relationship to that plan, you will realise that guidance is every-where. Accepting this, you will know that you are not travelling an isolated path without signposts or directions. You will realise that your soul and its allies, particularly those of dreams, guides and angels, are travelling alongside you at every moment of every day and every night.

Guidance and protection

The material of this chapter does not lend itself to a case history as such, but the following three stories will hopefully serve to illustrate further how your soul speaks through dreams, guides and angels.

Leonie: the guidance in a dream

This dream was dreamed by Leonie when she was ill with cancer and frightened about its outcome. Similar to A Dark Night Dream on page 158 this too, at first, has a nightmarish quality. It was also a repetitive dream.

Leonie recorded: 'I am being chased by three figures dressed in dark cloaks or robes and with dark hoods over their heads, obscuring their faces. I am terrified. I feel that these are aspects of my illness, trying to catch up with me and take me over. I run as fast as I can, but now they are gaining on me to the point at which on some nights I feel as though they are breathing down my neck and I will certainly not escape.'

Leonie had a strong belief that her illness was in some way a punishment. She felt guilty about what she saw as her shortcomings in life and felt that she had let her children, friends and family down, by not being adequate enough for them. She felt unready to die, because she hoped to take action to change her old patterns, but she did feel that the illness had her in its grasp and that she would not recover. Her own thoughts about this dream were that it confirmed that the illness would 'get her'. Leonie's therapist asked her to re-enter the dream, even though she was so terrified that the dark figures meant her some kind of harm. With dream therapy, where a dreamer is being chased, it is a common practice to ask the dreamer to stop running, turn around and challenge whatever it is that is giving pursuit. This was a hard thing for Leonie to do, but in a slightly altered state of consciousness she re-entered the dream. Instead of trying to run faster she stopped, turned around and asked the figures what they wanted of her. To her surprise the three figures threw back their cloaks and hoods to reveal that they were dazzling angelic beings. They apologised profusely to her for the fear they had caused, but explained that it was Leonie's belief in the power of her illness and that she needed it as some kind of punishment that had actually meant that she could only see darkness and not light and help. Their dark cloaks were her inability to see anything other than doom and gloom. They said, 'We are the angels of light and love and healing, and we have been trying to catch up with you. Try not to be afraid. All will be well.' It was an emotional moment. Leonie continued to work on her guilt theme and her sense that she needed to be punished and began to call on her angels of love, light and healing to help her treatment process. She had a lot to go through, as cancer patients so often have, but she did not die and lived many more years free of the disease and with a very full quality of life, free of the burdens of her guilt beliefs.

Thomas: a guide speaks

Thomas was in a dilemma about his future career. He was a healer, and had built up quite a busy practice, which he ran in addition to the full-time job he felt he needed in order to earn money to live. He accepted donations for his healing, but did not charge fees. He was becoming exhausted, working full time in a routine job as well as giving increasing time to his healing work. He reluctantly accepted that if he wanted his healing practice to be the main work of his life, he would have to consider charging fees and either work part-time at his routine job or give it up altogether and hope that he would still survive financially. It is a dilemma that many healers face. In one sense, healing is not a commodity that can be charged for, but eventually, if healers want to fulfil the demand for their work, they may have to accept that they need to charge for their time. As Thomas debated his dilemma, he received an unexpected offer of sponsorship that was very tempting. The sponsor was offering generous back-up support but wanted Thomas to sign a contract forming some kind of 'trust'. He was not happy with some of the terms of the contract, feeling that the sponsor, although generous, wanted to control almost every area of his life. He wondered though, whether this was a way through and might be just the sign he had been waiting and asking for. Thomas signed the contract, although he felt some reluctance and almost a sense of foreboding as he did so. It was not until he was at the post box with the signed contract and at the point of dropping it in, that a very loud voice in his head said 'Do not post that letter!' It was so dramatic that he pulled his hand away from the post box slot, letter still in hand, and went home to think things over again. Thomas had realised for some time that there was a guidance presence with him, especially when he was doing his healing work, and now this presence began to communicate more clearly. His guide explained that Thomas needed to trust his healing skills more, rather than getting tied up in a legal trust.

The sponsor was indeed trying, in his own way and with great generosity, to help Thomas forward, but indeed, he also wanted control. He would have tried to promote Thomas in a particular way and Thomas had always believed that his practice could grow 'organically'. He was still free to post his contract if he so wished, but the more he thought about it the more he saw unforeseen pitfalls in the commitment he had been on the brink of making. He thanked his potential sponsor, but decided to wait. As his practice grew, he gradually did his routine job less frequently and eventually was able to let it go. He knew that some of the material privations he had decided to undertake gave him a freedom and satisfaction with his own way of doing things that sponsorship would have denied him. His contact with his guide flourished increasingly as well, making him able to offer guidance to his clients as well as healing.

Isabel: a guardian angel steps in

Isabel learned to drive at a later age in life than most. To her surprise she mastered the lessons relatively easily and became a good and enthusiastic driver. She was delighted to have her own car, and in her free time and holidays went off to discover the parts of England, Wales, Scotland and Ireland she had always wanted to visit, loving the freedom to discover minor roads and the less frequented areas of the countryside. On one occasion she was driving down a steep and winding road, thoroughly enjoying the view. With hindsight she said, 'I should have stopped to enjoy it all properly, but I was anxious to find accommodation for the night.' The views were breathtaking and, as she rounded each corner, a new vista seemed to outdo the one before. She suddenly realised that the car was hurtling along at a speed that was unwise for the road she was driving on, with its constant bends. It seemed to be gathering more and more speed, even though she was attempting to brake. She became afraid that there was something wrong with the car and that it was out of control. Suddenly, the car seemed to be full of what she described as 'bright rainbow light' and a voice in her ear said urgently, 'Take your foot off the clutch!' Bemused by the views, she had not realised that her foot was on the clutch, not the brake, and the car was gathering momentum with the steep downward incline.

'My guardian angel was working overtime that day,' she said, as she told her story. I asked her why she was so sure that it was her guardian angel and not her guide. She said, 'The car was full of light, the voice was like a clear bell and when I stopped the car and pulled over to recover, I distinctly felt the sense of soft wings enfolding me.'

People often ask, 'How can I know who is communicating with me? Is it my soul, my dreaming self, my guide or my guardian angel?' The easiest of these to know, of course, is your dreaming self, the one who dreams your dreams and brings them to you as messages from your soul.

For the others, the differences between the places from which guidance comes are very subtle and there is a connection between all your wise guidance sources, who are allies of your soul.

In Exercises 7 (page 96), 8 (page 99) and 9 (page 117) mention is made of your inner wise presence or being. When you perceive your inner wise presence as a being, it often appears as an archetypal wise figure. You might equally experience it as a fragrance, a colour, a difference in wavelength or vibration, or as a sense of resonance coming from a consistent direction.

Discarnate guides may also be perceived in similar ways, although not so often as an archetypal wise figure. Discarnate guides often choose to appear as monks, Native Americans, Chinese, Egyptians, Atlanteans, or in other ancient forms. They take on a 'costume' that they feel you will recognise and warm towards. I first experienced Gildas as a monk in white robes, and he later explained that this was how he was dressed in his final incarnation on earth. I needed this vision and experience of him at that time, but now I sense his energy body as full of light, colour and fragrance, and I don't need him to have such a strong human identity or likeness.

Your inner wise presence might communicate from your heart centre area, in words, inferences or colours; your higher self/soul might give you a sense of inner knowing or realisation usually somewhere in the region of your crown or brow chakra (see Glossary); your spirit guide might give you symbols or clear words received into your brow chakra or your heart, but coming either from behind you, beside you, or directly in front of you; your guardian angel might touch you subtly with a sense of angelic wings or give you words that feel as if they are a clear bell note, which is of a higher or lighter tone than any subtly felt or heard voice of a spirit guide. As a general rule, angelic messages are usually quite short, whereas guides tend to give longer explanations.

At first it *is* difficult to know which is which, but given experience you will finally realise that there is a consistency of one sort or another that helps you to differentiate intuitively which source is which. The main thing is to be content to receive that which you differentiate as wisdom from another perspective or realm without worrying about its exact source but only about its quality.

Exercise on appreciation

Exercise 11 helps you to appreciate the care your guardian angel has taken of you during your life and the part it has played in keeping you in line with your soul contract. It offers you the opportunity to ask your guardian angel any questions that came to you during Exercise 10 (page 149). Before you begin, read through Preparing for the Exercises on page 5.

Exercise 11: *recognising the continual presence of your guardian angel in your life*

This is a meditative drawing and life-review exercise. Have your special notebook or sheets of paper and crayons, pastels or paints to hand so that you can use them right from the start, while in reflective mode.

1. Make sure that you will be comfortable and undisturbed. Find your comfortable position.

2. Focus on the rhythm of your breathing. Be aware of each in-breath and out-breath, do not try to alter your breath rhythm in any particular way, but allow it to find its natural level and flow.

3. Sense your breath as coming in and out at the 'petals' of your heart centre or chakra (life energy centre). This lies in the centre of your body and aura on the same level as your physical heart (see Glossary).

4. As your regular breathing helps your heart chakra to open, get a sense of entering your own inner space or dimension.

5. Ask that you might experience the feeling of your guardian

angel standing behind you and enfolding you in its light and in the high energy but softness of the vibration of its wings.

6. Using a full page, meditatively draw an outline of an angel shape in your special notebook or on a sheet of paper, using any colours or drawing effects you wish. (In all drawing exercises it does not matter if you are not accomplished in drawing. A roughly and simply sketched angelic shape is quite sufficient.)

7. When you have drawn the shape, start at the bottom left-hand corner of your drawing and think about anything you remember or have been told about your birth – your entry into incarnation. Your guardian angel was particularly present at this time. Write the word 'birth' in colour if you wish, and draw a small angel shape beside the word. Thank your guardian angel for watching over your entry into the world and for any special efforts it might have needed to make if you had a difficult or unusual birth.

8. Gradually work round the angel shape you have drawn, from the bottom left to the bottom right; thinking of the latter as where you are in your life now, and working through from your birth, to your childhood, to your adolescence, and to your adult life, recall events where you were at risk, in danger, had unusual experiences, adventures, made new choices or had things to celebrate. Whatever you experienced your guardian angel would have been present. If there were very difficult experiences in your life, try to sense that although you were not totally protected from these, your guardian angel might neverthe-less have helped them to be less terrible than they might have been and would have been giving you the strength to

come through and survive, or guiding you towards any necessary help you needed.

9. Work around the angel shape, drawing small angel 'icons' for each time that you sense your guardian angel was with you. Then close your eyes, and once again try to sense your angel's presence and its wings gently wrapped around you.

10. Ask the question of your guardian angel that you may have felt you wanted to ask in Exercise 10.

11. After about 10 minutes take a last look at what you have drawn and written. When you are ready, become conscious of the whole of your body and where you are sitting in your normal, everyday world.

12. Feel your contact with the ground, open your eyes and connect with your outer surroundings, before closing them again in order to visualise a cloak of light, with a hood, right around you.

This is the final exercise to use with the others given throughout the book. You will want to return to your records for all of them from time to time, as you use them to help you realise not only how you can work with your soul and how your soul works with you but also that you are securely within its guardianship, co-creativity and trust.

The next chapter summarises and concludes the book and looks again at the way in which individual soul work juxtaposes with the evolution of the human collective.

10

Your Soul's Evolution

Whether you seek the dimension of soul and meaning in life or not, you are working with your soul. Soul work cannot be avoided. Even if you do not have or want knowledge of higher perspectives, you are nevertheless working for, and with, your soul. Life is experience, and experience is what your soul both plans and seeks. You will take your life experience back to your soul whether you have consciously worked with a belief in soul as you lived your life, or not.

Lives lived with a minimum sense of awareness also contain a soul contract because your soul draws on every experience for its evolution. As a human being you are different from other species because you hold the ability to study, observe and speculate about the universe in which you live. As an individual personality bead linked to your soul's evolution you are part of the universe or cosmos of your soul and consciously or unconsciously are playing your part in its total evolution.

Spiritually, however, as this book has aimed to show, it is much more fulfilling to have greater awareness of your soul and its plans, agenda or contract, for your life, so that you can give life a greater sense of meaning. Learning to read, or decode your soul's agenda can be exciting, and when you take that path, whatever your circumstances in life, you will always feel accompanied. The exercises given at the end of each chapter form a series, and if you undertake them seriously and in sequence you will be following a path of spiritual growth and enabling yourself truly to live with a sense of soulful purpose.

The all-seeing and overseeing soul

Just as you cannot be in isolation from your soul, so your soul cannot be in isolation from other souls and groups of souls, as explained in Chapter 2. You, as an individual and incarnate bead from your soul thread, are playing a part in the total evolution of the family of humanity – which is *your* extended family.

Guides from the subtle planes tell us that we are gradually moving into a golden age. As you look at the general conditions in the world in which you live today, there may seem to be plenty of existential reasons to either doubt the dawn of a golden age or to assume that there is still a long way to go. When you are aware of what is going on in the world almost at the moment that it happens, you cannot but be very aware also of the depth and breadth of the shadow side of humanity. It is in making the shadow conscious that evolution happens, so another perspective might be to say, 'Indeed, I live in exciting times where there is a great deal of collective soul work to be done, and by working more actively with my soul I know that I am not only looking to my personal interests but also to those of the greater family of humanity.'

Making change

You might find inspiration in the interesting concept of the 'creative minority' or 'critical mass'. This asserts that when an optimum number of people change their behaviour or belief system, then the whole of humanity will change because of a subtle process known as morphic resonance. When enough people change then *all* people change. When *you* change you are contributing to the movement towards that optimum number that will bring about magical and instant change in the whole of humanity. The work you do by considering your own life and its relationship to something higher or more numinous is not only a work for yourself and your soul but for humanity and for the earth, and for the relationship of earth to other planets and bodies in our solar system and the universe.

As well as working on themes that relate to the evolution of your own soul, you work on themes that are connected to the evolution of the whole. Being a woman, or being a man, being religious or spiritual or a follower of the mundane, makes you part of a wider group within the whole. Some of your soul contract will be concerned not only with addressing your own karmic and evolutionary issues but also with being an ambassador for wider issues and themes of evolution within the whole body of humanity and its experience in the times in which you have chosen to live. The working out of what it means to be a man and what it means to be a woman, and the optimum creative relationship between them, is one of these wider issues of our times. Coping with difference in general is also one of these wider issues. Every day news bulletins are full of incidents concerning racial and ideological strife, which cannot help but affect every one of us. Yet it is in being aware of difficulty that we eventually find solutions. Personal soul work helps you to live in harmony with yourself, and when more people are able to do that, so the whole of humanity will learn to celebrate difference instead of fearing it.

Two dreams

You are in the midst of your own concerns but you are also an actor on the greater stage of life. Two clients had what I would call 'auditorium dreams'. These dreams give us a sense of individual and collective responsibility for evolution. They are each summed up within a sentence, but I include them here to help you enjoy two things: firstly, the personal wider and more meaningful perspective that learning to work in dialogue with your soul can give to your immediate life, and secondly, as an indication of your relationship at the same time to an even greater purpose – that of humanity evolving into its fullest potential.

The dreams speak to each of us and honour the way in which *your* soul work contributes to the greater whole.

The first dreamer dreamed, 'I am the Queen – I am beautiful and admired. I have many attendants but I am also aware that I have great responsibilities to fulfil.'

The second dreamer dreamed, 'I have a theatre in my house. Plays on interesting themes are put on and well acted and attract large audiences. We shall soon have to look for a bigger theatre in order to give many more the opportunity to see the importance of what is being enacted.'

Working more consciously with your soul will bring you personal fulfilment and put your life in meaningful context, but in the wider picture, it cannot be undertaken lightly. We are all responsible to each other, and soul work will bring you to that serious realisation. It will also open up the exciting opportunity for you to become more consciously a part of the spiritual evolution of humanity and to know yourself as a co-worker for the establishment of a golden age.

Can there be a better reason for taking on, in full awareness, the complex, hard, but thrilling journey of working with your soul?

GLOSSARY

Alchemy This is a tradition which originated in Persia. In Europe in the Middle Ages, alchemists were seen as being engaged on research which would enable lead (base metal) to be transformed into gold. Undoubtedly some, usually called 'puffers and blowers', undertook such research. However, true spiritual alchemy uses the imagery of base metal being transformed into gold as a basis for complex esoteric teaching about the journey and evolution of the soul.

Angelic Beings These are different reflections of Divine Consciousness. They are intermediaries and guardians helping the Divine plan to manifest on earth. Their hierarchy includes Guardian Angels, Archangels, Cherubim, Seraphim, Thrones and Powers. The angelic lifestream may be seen as moving from the divine consciousness out towards earth and humanity. The human stream of consciousness which includes discarnate guides, may be seen to be moving towards reunification with the Divine. Thus the angelic hierarchy is separate from humanity. Discarnates are not angels and angels will not take on human form or consciousness. When we die we will become discarnate, not angelic. Our Guardian Angels are thus different from our guides or discarnate mentors.

Archetypes/Archetypal forces By dictionary definition these are 'primordial images inherited by all'. Each human society is affected by forces such as peace, war, beauty, justice, wisdom, healing, death, birth, love and power – sometimes called the *archetypes of higher qualities*. The essence of these defies definition and we need images, myths, symbols and personifications to help us in understanding their breadth and depth. Tarot cards which have ancient origins, have 22 personified or symbolised archetypes of the major arcana. These cover all aspects of human experience.

Astrology This is the study of the planets in our solar system and how their positions and interactions affect us as human beings, both individually and collectively. The date of your birth gives you a 'sun sign': Aries, Taurus, Gemini, Cancer, Leo, Virgo, Libra, Scorpio, Sagittarius, Capricorn, Aquarius or Pisces. Popular horoscopes in magazines give weekly or daily predictions for 'life, love and luck', based on these sun signs. Personal astrological readings by experienced astrologers take into account the exact moment of your birth and calculate the position of all the planets at that moment in order to 'read' how they would be likely to affect your strengths, weaknesses and your journey through life. Your soul chooses the moment of your birth very carefully to ensure that you are born at the right astrological moment that will enhance your soul's task for you in your present incarnation.

Aura/auric field The energy field which interpenetrates with, and radiates out beyond, the physical body. Clairvoyantly seen, the aura is full of light, colour and shade. The trained healer or seer senses indications within the aura as to the spiritual, mental, physical and emotional state of the individual. Much of the auric colour and energy come from the chakras.

Chakras The word 'chakrum' is Sanskrit and means 'wheel'. Properly speaking, 'chakrum' is the singular form and 'chakra' the plural but in the West it is usual to speak of one chakra and several chakras. Much of the colour and energy of the auric field is supplied by the chakras. Clairvoyantly seen, they are wheels of light and colour interpenetrating with, affecting, and affected by, the physical body. Charkas carry links to specific parts of the glandular system and might therefore be described as subtle glands. Most Eastern traditions describe a sevenfold major chakra system, at the same time acknowledging varying large numbers of minor chakras. The names of the major chakras are: The Crown (at the crown of the head); The Brow (above and between the eyes); The Throat (at the centre of the neck); The Heart (in the centre of the body on the same level as the physical heart); The Solar Plexus (centrally, just under the rib cage); The Sacral (two fingers below the navel); and the Root (in the perineum area). Working with the chakras aids physical, mental, and spiritual health. The seven major chakras carry the colours of the rainbow spectrum: red for the Root, orange for the Sacral, yellow for the Solar Plexus, green for the Heart, blue for the Throat, indigo for the Brow and violet for the Crown.

Findhorn in Scotland is one of the oldest established spiritual communities where, particularly during the 1960s, it was discovered that the growth of plants and vegetables can be significantly influenced and improved by communicating and cooperating with their life force. Courses for those who feel ready to explore spiritual teaching and self-growth are run as part of the work of the community. There is also a Findhorn press, which publishes spiritual and esoteric books.

Healing is the art and practice of channelling energy to help the body to heal itself of ailments and diseases. Certain people are gifted with the ability to heal, but to some extent it can also be learned by or trained in almost each one of us. Some healers 'lay on hands', others focus more in the auric field and the chakras. Healing can help with mental and emotional conditions as well as physical ones. The medical profession is increasingly accepting that healers can have a beneficial effect on many conditions and in some places healers are beginning to be officially employed by the NHS.

Higher self Your higher self is part and parcel of your soul and is considered to be the voice of the consciousness that oversees, processes and makes choices for the many facets of your incarnate life and existence. Your soul, your spirit and your higher self are interactive subtle aspects of your greater or wider being.

Inner wise being or presence In our good moments when we make clear decisions or give wise, non-judgemental advice to a friend, we know that we have access to a place of wisdom within. It has little to do with personal experience and is related to a knowledge of inner potential and the potential of humankind. In inner journeys this source of wisdom may become personified. It may appear as a mythological or archetypal being or animal; it may simply be experienced as an atmosphere of sacredness and love, a fragrance, a colour, a difference in vibration or a sense of resonance coming from a consistent direction. By learning that in the inner worlds we can call this being or presence to us as at will, we can be led to deeper layers of self-understanding as well as be empowered to use its strength more often more consciously in outer life.

Karma is the spiritual law of cause and effect (which defies 'nutshell' definition.) 'As you sow, so shall you reap' is a basic but over-simplified definition. Belief in karma goes alongside belief in reincarnation and personal, progressive evolution. The tendency is to see karma as being something troublesome or heavy which needs to be overcome during a specific lifetime – but giftedness or innate wisdom are also positive karmic attributes.

Other planes, realms or spheres When incarnate, our existence is dependent upon the material plane, where things have substance and solidity. Yet we are complex beings and if we pause to consider the range of our perceptions, not all can be explained by the laws of physics. Many people encounter 'other worldly phenomena' from near death experiences to prophetic dreams, from sensing 'atmospheres' in old buildings to telepathic communication with a loved one, either alive or dead.

Esoteric teaching tells us that there are at least six other planes of experience, which are not just phenomena of perception but actual territories. The nearest to us is the etheric plane, which in itself is largely an interface between the material and the astral plane. This latter is divided into a number of layers or regions. The lower astral is largely populated with negative thought forms. (It is probably the regions which severe alcoholics and drug users experience when they have the DT's or a bad trip). The higher levels of the astral plane are where we meet our guides and where there are temples of light, colour and healing and beautiful, subtle landscapes. We may visit the astral planes in our dreams each night, as well as being able to travel there in the altered state of consciousness induced by meditation. Beyond the astral plane are the feeling plane, the lower and higher mental planes, the causal plane and the ketheric plane. (Names for each of the planes may vary to some extent from teacher to teacher, those used here are given by Gildas.)

Power animal The concept of the power animal has its roots in Shamanistic and Native American lore. Animals can help us in our inner worlds. They protect us, guide us, mirror lessons for us, and help us to stay in contact with our natural sense of what is right, wholesome and safe. With their aid, in our inner worlds we can see in the dark, swim under water whilst still breathing, fly and glide on air currents, walk through fire and survive the swamp or the pit. The strong yet gentle power animals of our inner worlds may be very wild or fierce in the outer. When we cross the threshold to inner experience they become our friends, they may speak to us and become our guides, guardians, way-showers and protectors.

It is possible to meet unfriendly animals in our inner worlds or dreams. In this case they usually symbolise some inner conflict or imbalance, but the true power animal can always be trusted, will come when we call, track us when we stray, energise us when we are fatigued and help to heal us when we are ill. They are recognised by the light in their eyes and their joy at being found by us, or invited into the journey.

Psychology is the study of human nature, with all its drives and experiences.

Soul or Spiritual Family In the organisation of souls, we are divided into groups and families. When other members of our spiritual or soul family are in incarnation with us we usually 'recognise' them and form deep and inspiring friendships or relationships with them. The genetic family into which we are born does not necessarily contain members of our spiritual family. Children, parents, siblings may be very different in soul nature and origin. We may not find our true soul family until comparatively late in life.

Soul mates The soul thread has two strands, like a double-stranded necklace joined at the clasp. Soul mates are personality beads, incarnate at the same time as you, from the same thread as yourself, and on the same strand.

Soul service Something such as the call or will to teach, nurse, or practice law.

Soul work encompasses the whole of life and the way you live it.

Source Used rather than a more religious and masculine or paternal term such as 'God'. The Source is Divine, the planner of the universe, the origin of all life. It incorporates masculine and feminine principles equally

Spiritual growth includes the search for higher meaning and purpose in life.

Spiritual teacher or guide/Gildas/Channelling A spiritual teacher can be any mentor who helps us address the soul, spiritual and philosophic aspects of living, being and existing and inspires our search for meaning. In this book when I refer to my spiritual teacher or discarnate guide, I am speaking of a being who inhabits the subtle planes and who I know as 'Gildas'. Such guides have been through many lifetimes or incarnations and are now working from another dimension. By a slight shift of consciousness I can be in touch with Gildas, feel his presence and mentally hear/register his words and teaching. I can then speak out, or write down, what I am being told. This is a form of spiritual channelling or mediumship. Increasing numbers of people today are discovering their ability to channel.

Subtle bodies Beyond our physical body, forming the auric field, are subtle bodies or energy layers, each having a different frequency or vibration. Through these bodies, links with our soul and higher and wider being are maintained and remembered. At death the subtle bodies live on and 'clothe' our spirits as they pass to the other side. The total number of subtle bodies accepted by most sources is six. (That is seven bodies altogether when the physical body is included). Terminology for these bodies varies from source to source. The terminology Gildas uses in his teaching is, moving out from the physical, the etheric body, the astral body, the feeling body, the lower mental body, the higher mental body, and the ketheric, soul, or causal body.

The mystical marriage When your soul has processed all it has learned through incarnation, its purpose is complete and the soul and spirit have attained a marriage which is known as the mystical marriage.

Twin soul The soul thread has two strands, like a double-stranded necklace joined at the clasp. Each thread has personality beads. Twin souls are personality beads from the parallel thread. During incarnations, a bead from one of your soul strands may meet with a bead from its twin strand. This is the meeting that brings about the incarnate experience of meeting with a twin soul or perfect partner. Beads from your twin soul strand may be your parents, grandparents, children or grandchildren as well as your perfect mate or life partner.

Yin and yang These are Chinese words for the basic but opposite aspects necessary to creation. Yin is receptive, feminine and dark. Yang is active, masculine and light. In the traditional yin/yang symbol, one black and one white fish-like shape nestle together within a perfect circle. The eye of the black shape is white and the eye of the white shape is black, showing that the seed of each is contained in the other.

FURTHER READING

Books by Ruth White
A Message of Love, Piatkus Books, 1994
A Question of Guidance, C.W. Daniel Co. Ltd, 1989
Energy Healing For Beginners, Piatkus Books, 2002
Gildas Communicates (with Mary Swainson), C.W Daniel Co. Ltd, 1971
Karma and Reincarnation, Piatkus Books, 2000
Seven Inner Journeys (with Mary Swainson), C.W. Daniel Co. Ltd, 1975
The Healing Spectrum (with Mary Swainson), C.W. Daniel Co. Ltd, 1979
The River of Life: A Guide to Your Spiritual Journey, Piatkus Books, 1997
Using Your Chakras: A New Approach to Healing Your Life, Piatkus Books, 2000
Working With Guides and Angels, Piatkus Books, 2006
Working With Spirit Guides, Piatkus Books, 2004
Working With Your Chakras, Piatkus Books, 2007

Other titles
Bailey, Alice, *Discipleship in the New Age*, Lucis Press Ltd, 1972
Cooper, CJ, *An Illustrated Encyclopaedia of Traditional Symbols,* Thames and Hudson, 1979
Ferrucci, Pierro, (Disciple of Assagioli), *What We May Be,* Jeremy P. Tarcher, 2000
Garfield, Patricia, *The Dream Book, A Young Person's Guide to*

FURTHER READING

Understanding Dreams, McClelland & Stewart Inc, 2002
Jung, C.G., *Man and His Symbols,* Picador, 1978
Hillman, James, *The Soul's Code,* Bantam, 1997
Kaplan, Connie, *Dreams are Letters from The Soul,* Harmony Books, 2002
Moore, Thomas, *Dark Nights of the Soul,* Piatkus Books, 2004
Mosse, Kate, *Labyrinth,* Orion Books, 2005

Packs of inspirational symbolic cards:
(There are many of these, but here is a selection)
Franklin, Anna, *The Celtic Animal Oracle,* Vega, 2003
Franzani, Lianne, *Dolphin Affirmations,* Koppenhol Publishing Company B.V., 2003
Lerner, Mark and Lerner, Isha, *Inner Child Cards,* Bear and Co, 2002
Sams, Jamie and Carson, David, *Medicine Cards,* Bear and Co, 1999
Virtue, Doreen, *Messages From Your Angels* Oracle Cards, Hay House, 2002
Virtue, Doreen, *Magical Unicorns,* Oracle Cards, Hay House, 2005

INDEX